P9-CQM-268

BEYOND
LEAF
RAKING

"Everyone can be great
because everyone can serve."

—Dr. Martin Luther King, Jr.

BEYOND LEAF RAKING

LEARNING TO SERVE / SERVING TO LEARN

Peter L. Benson
and
Eugene C. Roehlkepartain

Abingdon Press
Nashville

BEYOND LEAF RAKING:
LEARNING TO SERVE/SERVING TO LEARN

Copyright © 1993 by Search Institute

This book is printed on recycled, acid-free paper.

Library of Congress Cataloging-in-Publication Data

Benson, Peter L.
    Beyond leaf raking : learning to serve/serving to learn / Peter L. Benson,
Eugene C. Roehlkepartain.
      p.   cm. — (Essentials for Christian youth)
    Includes bibliographical references.
    ISBN 0-687-21328-2 (alk. paper)
    1. Church group work with youth. 2. Youth in church work. 3. Experiential learning.
I. Roehlkepartain, Eugene C., 1962–   .
II. Title. III. Series.
BV4447.B469   1993
259'.23—dc20
                                                            93-28845

99 00 01 02 — 10 9

Photo Credits:
Jean-Claude Lejeune—pages 13, 25, 35, 54, 63, 76, 85, 99.
Jim West—pages 8, 106.

Figure 1 and excerpts from *Giving and Volunteering Among American Teenagers 12 to 17 Years of Age*, published by Independent Sector in 1992, are reprinted by permission of the publisher.
   Figure 2 and material reprinted from *Organizational Psychology* by David Kolb, published by Prentice Hall in 1974, are used by permission of the publisher.
   Figures 9, 10, 13, and related material are from *Combining Service and Learning: A Resource Book for Community and Public Service,* edited by Jane C. Kendall and Associates and published by the National Society for Experiential Education in 1990. Reprinted by permission of the publisher.
   Figure 11, and all quotations and references from National Youth Leadership Council publications are used with the permission of NYLC.
   Figure 5 and excerpts from *Experiential Education and the Schools*, edited by Richard Kraft and James Kielmeier, and published in 1986 by Association for Experiential Education, are used by permission of the publisher.
   Excerpts from *Christian Religious Education* by Thomas H. Groome, Copyright © 1980 by Thomas H. Groome, are reprinted by permission of HarperCollins Publishers, Inc.

Dedication

To our children,
Liv, Kai, and Micah

MANUFACTURED IN THE UNITED STATES OF AMERICA

Contents

98412

List of Figures

Acknowledgments

This work represents our gathering of the collected wisdom of many people across the country. Thanks to the following people who took time to tell their stories and share their insights about service in congregations. Without them, this resource would not be as rich.

- Jeff Allee, Kirkwood Baptist Church, Kirkwood, Missouri
- David Ashworth, Anderson Hills United Methodist Church, Cincinnati, Ohio
- David Carver, Twelve Corners Presbyterian Church, Rochester, New York
- Beverly CroweTipton, Seventh and James Baptist Church, Waco, Texas
- Dean Feldmeyer, Faith United Methodist Church, Canal Winchester, Ohio
- Philip Hannam, Zion Baptist Church, Minneapolis, Minnesota
- Sally Johnson, Seminary Consortium for Urban Pastoral Education (SCUPE), Chicago, Illinois
- Deb Kielsmeier, National Youth Leadership Council, St. Paul, Minnesota
- Dick Lundy, St. Luke Presbyterian Church, Wayzata, Minnesota
- Margaret Rickers Hinchey, Our Father Lutheran Church, Denver, Colorado
- Walt Marcum, Highland Park United Methodist Church, Dallas, Texas
- Karen McKinney, National Youth Leadership Council, St. Paul, Minnesota
- Greg Dobie Moser, Catholic Diocese of Columbus, Ohio
- Mike Nygren, Ginghamsburg United Methodist Church, Tipp City, Ohio.
- Carol Davis Younger, College Heights Baptist Church, Manhattan, Kansas

To guide us as we prepared this manuscript, we have relied upon the writings of pioneers and leaders and activists in the field of service-learning and community ministry. Some of these people are friends we have personally known and respected; others, we have come to know and respect through their work: Dan Conrad, Carl Dudley, the late Diane Hedin, James Kielsmeier, Jane Kendall, and Kate McPherson. Our deep appreciation to each of these leaders for laying the foundation for this book.

We also express our appreciation to the following people in the fields of service-learning, youth ministry, and community ministry. They carefully reviewed this manuscript and made important suggestions: Faye Caskey, Sally Johnson, Deb Kielsmeier, Kate McPherson, and Carol Davis Younger.

Our colleagues at Search Institute also assisted greatly with this project, through research, computer analysis, administrative support, and picking up some of the slack while we wrote: Dale A. Blyth, Richard Gordon, Amy Lash Esau, Rebecca N. Saito, Marilyn J. Erickson, and Adell M. Smith.

Finally, we thank Jill Reddig, our editor at Abingdon Press, for believing in this project, pushing us to finish it, and scrupulously maintaining quality. We couldn't have done it without you, Jill.

INTRODUCTION: INTEGRATING SERVICE AND LEARNING INTO YOUTH MINISTRY

Imagine a typical committee night at, say, Redeemer Community Church. Meetings started fifteen minutes ago, so the various committees are about to get down to business.

In the library, the Christian education committee is meeting. The group's agenda tonight is fairly similar to its agenda for every meeting in recent memory. Curriculum needs to be ordered. Teachers need to be found. Supplies need to be purchased. Budgets need to be cut.

But this night, the discussion turns philosophical. Seeking some perspective, one committee member wonders out loud how to address the underlying problems that plague the program. Her particular interest is the youth program. "Kids seem bored, apathetic, regardless of the curriculum we choose—it doesn't seem to make much difference." After a long pause, she finally concludes, "I just wonder sometimes if anything we're doing in our classes is having much of an impact on our young people."

Down the hall in an adult classroom is the missions/outreach committee. The committee chair shares a long list of requests for support and involvement. The food pantry is having a canned-food drive. The homeless shelter needs volunteers. The denomination's relief agency needs emergency funds. The local minister's council is sponsoring a CROP Walk and needs walkers and coordinators. A social-action group wants members to write letters to Congress and the president.

The chair drops the stack on the table with a sigh. "These are all good things, but we're maxed out already." Everyone around the table nods in agreement. After all, each of them has personally taken the lead on every benevolence project the church has undertaken.

Perhaps it's in the decaf that night, but one of these committee members becomes philosophical too. "It doesn't make sense," he asserts, "that a church can't get people to be involved in service and social justice. I get so tired of begging people to do things that I think should be a natural part of our faith."

It's a pity that those two committees weren't meeting together (or at least able to hear each other through the divider walls). Maybe a light bulb would come on as they realized that they were talking about similar problems—and that they could combine their energies to deal with their concerns in an innovative way through service-learning in their youth ministry.

"Service-learning? I've never heard of it!"

Unfortunately, perhaps no one on either committee had ever thought about—or heard of—service-learning. While it is a natural strategy for the church, it's largely an effort that's occurring in schools across the country. Service-learning uses service as an educational method. By integrating the experience of service into the classroom, it increases the relevance of course content for the real world. While the student grows by being able to make a significant difference, the community benefits by receiving the service.

Introduction

For at least two decades, educators and researchers have been studying and experimenting and evaluating and learning what works and what doesn't. And they have discovered many keys to success. They've learned about roadblocks. They've made mistakes and have tried to learn from them. They have success stories that regularly make the newspapers, and they've become quite effective in advocating their approach in school systems and in government. In fact, as we write this, the idea of community service has gained national attention (and scrutiny) because of the Clinton administration's national service agenda.

But, with a few exceptions, little of this learning has made its way into the church or youth ministry. The journals and magazines don't mention it. It's not on the agenda of youth-ministry training events. Books about it are virtually nonexistent.

Most telling, though, is what's happening (or not happening) in local congregations. Young people gather in classrooms to read and discuss (or hear lectures about) scripture, and to watch videos on theology, personal issues, and social concerns. In the summer, they may go on a mission trip or to a work camp. But rarely are connections made between what they talk about in the classroom and what they do in the community.

Karen McKinney has a unique perspective on this. Now on the staff of National Youth Leadership Council—a leader in service-learning—she formerly ran a youth-leadership program in an urban Minneapolis congregation. "A lot of service happens in the churches," she says, "but they miss the learning. . . . Tons of churches will have kids do service . . . but they miss the reflection piece." She adds: "Service just becomes something good to do. The learning that comes from it is accidental."

At the same time, Search Institute's research on youth, adults, and leaders in five mainline denominations indicates that relatively few youths are involved in direct service to others through their congregations. Only 29 percent of Protestant young people has spent 11 or more hours in a congregation-sponsored service project *in their lifetime.* Furthermore, when pastors were asked about what their congregations emphasize, service and social action were at the bottom of the list of 22 possibilities.

These realities reflect a significant missed opportunity for congregations. Serving others is not only a central demand of the gospel, but being involved in serving others has positive values for youth. Young people who serve others are less likely to be involved in at-risk behaviors, and they are more likely to develop the kind of prosocial value orientation that carries over into choice-making, career selection, and empathy for others. Furthermore, direct service is an invaluable experiential learning opportunity in which young people can internalize their faith.

A Growing Awareness and Concern

The good news is that some of these realities may be shifting. Much has been made about the decade of the 1990s moving away from the excesses of the 1980s. Young people, the pundits tell us, are more concerned about others and more concerned about their world. The environment has become the issue of the day, and young people are beginning to be given more responsibility. Even the presidential campaign of 1992 elevated the issue of service to top priority, in partial response to the cultural shift away from community and toward individualism.[1]

The same shift may be occurring in the church. Religious publishers from across the spectrum have introduced books on the environment and other social issues. People who run work camps and missions indicate growing participation in their programs. And a survey of 100 youth-ministry denominational executives and experts by Group Publishing found that "developing youth as servants" was one of the 5 top concerns, with 8 out of 10 respondents indicating that this ranks "high" or "very high" as a top issue for youth workers in the 1990s.[2]

The danger in all this, however, is that the church will spend the next twenty years making the same mistakes and reinventing the same wheels that public-school educators have been addressing and refining. That's why we've written *Beyond Leaf Raking:* to help youth ministers, Christian educators, social-ministry coordinators, and others in the church learn to apply the service-learning model to youth ministry. We see it as a perfect match that can reinvigorate Christian education programs, stimulate youth involvement in service and social action, and build bonds of interest between youth and the congregations.

So, What *Is* Service-Learning?

Few congregations call anything they do "service-learning," but many are already using elements of it. Some might call it mission education or experiential education or faith in action or shared praxis or action-reflection. The language isn't nearly as important as the idea.

Consider this definition of service-learning offered by James C. Kielsmeier, one of the leaders in the movement: "Service-Learning is a way of combining the methods of experiential education with the needs of society. It is serving and learning, and it is a way of creating the world. Young people need real employment and real service opportunities—and communities need genuine work and service accomplished."[3]

Service-learning happens in the youth group that spends a week rebuilding homes in Appalachia and spends the evenings—and the weeks that follow—reflecting on its lifestyle, faith commitments, and Christian responsibilities for people in poverty.

Service-learning happens in the confirmation class that learns about the elements of Christian worship by preparing and leading a worship service in a nursing home or prison.

Service-learning happens in the Sunday school class that prepares a guide on issues in an upcoming election—with its understanding of the impact of the issues on the church's commitments—and distributes it in the congregation.

Service-learning happens in the youth group that runs a hotline for other young people who need a listening ear, and has regular training sessions to learn caring skills and ways to address specific problems.

Service-learning happens in the youth group that initiates a peer-counseling program, teaching young people how to care for one another and helping them process these experiences in faith terms.

Service-learning happens when a teenager spends Thursday afternoons tutoring at the elementary school, then reflects on that experience in Sunday school three days later.

Service-learning happens in the family that serves soup in the homeless shelter and uses the experience as the catalyst for rethinking family priorities and spending habits.

Service-learning happens in the youth group that researches and writes a drama about the environment to encourage other churches to take care of creation.

In short, service-learning occurs in youth ministry when service and learning are intertwined in ways that express Christian love and commitment, while also deepening that commitment through reflection and study. Service-learning is a wholistic approach to learning which begins with doing and choosing, then moves to thinking and feeling—a natural way to learn.

Service-learning is not a particular program or particular type of project. Rather, it's a way of thinking and doing and growing—a life-style of servanthood that permeates all aspects of the youth ministry. In some traditions, it builds on a "missions" emphasis. In others, it may build on a "social ministry" or "outreach" emphasis. Whatever the specific language, the goal is essentially the same.

What We Bring to This Book

We are convinced that service-learning has great potential for the congregation. As David Ashworth, minister of education and youth at Anderson Hill United Methodist Church in Cincinnati told us, "It seems like we have more of a mandate to be serving, rather than just letting the public schools do that. . . . We ought to be ahead of the schools."

We at Search Institute chose to write this book because it brings together several important themes in our research about children and youth:

- First is our 35-year commitment to quality research about youth in religious organizations. Most recently we completed the Effective Christian Education study, in which we examined characteristics of Christian-education programs for youth and adults in six denominations. That study pointed to troubling realities in congregations and in youth programs, while also suggesting some of the potential remedies. The service-learning approach is one worthy approach to these findings.[4]
- A second theme in our work has been research to understand which values, beliefs, behaviors, and other factors in life help young people to grow up healthy. A recent study, *The Troubled Journey*, involves 47,000 sixth- through twelfth-graders in public schools and is the basis for some of the new research presented in this volume. This research underscores the value of service involvement in young people's lives.[5]
- The third theme concerns Search Institute's ongoing work as the major evaluator of a national service-learning initiative of the National Youth Leadership Council, one of the leaders in the school-based service-learning movement. Our work with this organization has immersed us in the research and practice of service-learning, and has allowed us to focus energy on the benefits and potential of this movement.
- Fourth is Search Institute's commitment to turning sometimes complex research findings into practical resources that will be useful to people who work with youth.

Each of these influences will be evident throughout this book. We begin by giving a brief overview of what the research tells us about the importance and impact of service-learning. We seek to present this information in a way that is useful and understandable.

But that's only the beginning. The bulk of the book builds on this research to provide practical, hands-on information about how to set up an effective service-learning program in a congregation, based on interviews, research, and stories of successful efforts in schools and congregations across the country. And we have provided worksheets, checklists, and guidelines throughout.

It's always hard to know how a book will be used. The reality is probably somewhere between the writer's dream of changing the world and the writer's nightmare that the book will gather dust in a bookstore. Our hope is that *Beyond Leaf Raking* will become a stimulator and guide not only to help communication between committees on missions and Christian-education, but to help service-learning become instrumental in nurturing faith among today's youth.

1 | A CALL TO SERVICE

In recent years, most of the headlines we've read about teenagers haven't been positive. We see stories about drugs and sexual activity and gangs and dropouts. Then, over coffee, we talk about all the problems we're having with our kids, warning parents with younger children that the "terrible twos" are nothing compared to the storms of adolescence. And we half-jokingly offer sympathy to parents who have teenagers.

The stories and conversations all feed into our images of adolescence as a disease—something to be avoided and, if contracted, cured as quickly as possible.

But from time to time, we see other stories that rattle our preconceptions: "Teens Top Adults in Volunteer Work"; "Youth Group Rebuilds Homes"; "Local Teens Tutor Young Children in Reading"; "Youth Lobbies Congress to Clean Up Environment." Underlying those headlines is a reemerging story of young people who are contributing in significant ways to our churches and communities.

In reality, the two sets of headlines are actually related. There's strong evidence that if we work to increase the number of stories in the second set, about youth becoming active in service, we're likely to see fewer headlines about their problem behaviors. And we believe that the church is a natural place for young people to become involved in service and social concerns—if only youth ministries would take advantage of the opportunities.

Why Get Youth Involved in Service?

One of the ongoing debates in youth-ministry circles concerns the role of service, or outreach. Many argue that it is inappropriate to put much emphasis here, since youth programs should focus on "meeting young people's needs." If teenagers aren't interested in serving or taking social action, the argument goes, we shouldn't try to force them into it. After all, pushing them might just push them out of the church altogether. We ought to focus on helping them build positive friendships and a solid faith now; they can do the action stuff later. Proponents of these arguments point to the dismal attendance at service projects or in discussion groups about world issues as the ultimate confirmation that their perspective is accurate.

On some levels, the arguments are solid. It *is* important to meet youths' needs. It *is* important to keep teenagers interested and involved in the church. It *is* important to nurture young people's faith. And, yes, service projects and discussions of social issues can have dismal participation.

BUT . . .

None of those points contradicts a strong emphasis on service and social issues in youth ministry. In fact, those same goals also are attainable through a well-planned service-learning effort in the congregation. Instead of being an obstacle to youth involvement and growth in faith, involvement in service actually enhances these goals and increases youth ministry's impact on young people. Indeed, research on youth, current realities in our culture, and key themes in the Christian faith underscore the importance of service and social concerns for youth ministry.

The Biblical Mandate

Many other books have presented detailed, convincing evidence that service and justice are central themes in the Christian faith.[1] But even a casual reading of scripture makes the mandate virtually unavoidable for Christians who take scripture seriously. Jesus' life modeled one of service, compassion, and concern for the oppressed. Care for the needy was central to the life of the early church. And the prophets railed against the oppression and injustice all around them as despicable in the sight of God.

A quick survey of the Gospels highlights the centrality of service in Jesus' ministry. Beginning with John the Baptist's call to share whatever we have with others, through the range of Jesus' healing ministry, to the washing of the disciples' feet, to his parables about the kingdom, we see Jesus living life as a servant and calling his followers to walk in his footsteps.

Some might argue that, though they are good things, service and justice are not central to the gospel of salvation and grace. And, these people may continue, youth ministry should focus on the personal side of faith; the other can come later. Writing to people who claim this argument and perspective, Anthony Campolo makes the point this way:

> A church which provides its young people with opportunities and challenges for social change gives them the opportunity to explore some of the primary reasons for their salvation. Through these activities they will come to see that Jesus is not only interested in saving them from sin and getting them into heaven, but also wants to make them into instruments through which He can do His work in the world.[2]

Young people need to discover the full meaning of the faith—not save some parts of it for later. If we accept that action and service are imperatives of the faith, then it becomes imperative that they be central elements of ministry with youth.

Impact on Youth

In addition to the biblical mandate for service, becoming involved in service also has tremendous potential for helping young people grow up in healthy ways. Research by Search Institute and others suggests that active involvement in service has a number of impacts on young people.

- *Service involvement bonds youth to the church,* solidifying commitment and loyalty to the congregation. Young people who are active in service through the congregation are twice as likely as others to have strong ties to the congregation.
- *Service involvement is a key factor in nurturing young people's growth in faith.* In fact, service appears to be more powerful in nurturing faith than is Sunday school, Bible study, or participation in worship. This is true because, as Faye Caskey, a religious educator with experience in service-learning, says, "We behave ourselves into thinking and feeling more quickly than we feel ourselves into behaving."
- *Service involvement promotes healthy life-styles and choices among teenagers.* Young people who serve others are less likely to become involved in at-risk behaviors. They also develop positive self-esteem, self-confidence, and social skills. They see themselves as significant in the lives of others. According to an Independent Sector survey of teenagers who volunteer, young people say that their most important benefits from service are that they learned to respect

others, gained satisfaction from helping others, learned to be helpful and kind, learned how to get along with and relate to others, and learned new skills (see Figure 1).

- *Service involvement rewards young people with new skills and perspectives.* This value can be particularly important in working with youth who have few other opportunities to develop skills and interests, such as those in low-income urban areas.
- *Finally, people who become involved in service and justice when they are children or teenagers are much more likely to be involved in these issues when they become adults.* Thus this early leadership and experience in serving others plants seeds that bear fruit for a lifetime.

Figure 1
What Teens Gain from Volunteering

I learned to respect others.	48%
I gained satisfaction from helping others.	46%
I learned to be helpful and kind.	45%
I learned how to get along with and relate to others.	40%
I learned new skills.	37%
I learned to understand people who are different from me.	35%
I learned how to relate to children.	35%
I developed leadership skills.	34%
I'm a better person now.	33%
I'm more patient with others.	33%

According to an Independent Sector survey of teenagers who volunteer, here are the top benefits they say they receive from their activities. Percentages indicate the number of teenagers who say each benefit is "very important" to them.[3]

Each of these benefits for youth will be explored in more depth in chapter 2, which focuses on the potential impact of service-learning on young people. But the true impact of these experiences comes home when teenagers tell their stories of how service has changed their lives.

For many young people, the world is confined to the narrow walls of their neighborhood and experience. This might mean that an inner-city child has never seen a farm or climbed a mountain. Or it might mean that a suburban child has never seen a homeless person. When service occurs across boundaries—be they economic, racial, ethnic, educational, age, religious, or geographic—young people grow in their understanding of the diversity of the world. An excerpt from the journal of a youth involved in a nursing home illustrates the impact:

I remember my first days at Oak Terrace. I was scared to touch people, or the doorknobs even. And I used to wash my hands after I left there every single day! Can you believe it? Now I go and get big hugs and kisses from everyone. Get this—I even eat there! That's a horror story for some people.[4]

Impact on the Youth Group

The positive impact of service involvement is not limited to individual teenagers. In promotional literature from many of the national work camp programs, you notice that these service events are primarily touted for their ability to "build community in your youth group." And while it's difficult to find research to confirm the positive impact of service on youth groups, reports from congregations support the marketing claims. Youth workers regularly attribute improved group cohesion and commitment to service projects. And there's some evidence that a strong service program can result in numerical growth as well.

For example, consider the experience of Ginghamsburg United Methodist Church. While most youth programs see about two-thirds of the young people become inactive in grades ten through twelve, the Ginghamsburg church keeps almost all its young people actively involved throughout high school. And in the twelve years since the service emphasis began in the youth program, the group's size has grown from about 60 to 200 active participants.

When asked what keeps young people involved, Youth Pastor Mike Nygren doesn't hesitate: "They come to be with their friends." Because the church draws youth from 15 to 20 schools across the metropolitan Dayton area, the youth program works hard to build a sense of community. But, Nygren notes, the church does it with service projects instead of pizza parties and outings to football games.

In fact, service has many key ingredients for building a strong, cohesive youth ministry. And while, to date, research to verify the impact is limited, the patterns emerge in the stories.

A Shared Task and Purpose—A shared task is the beginning of team process. When young people work together, sharing the challenges, struggles, and successes, they grow closer. It gives them something common to talk about. And when they leave their own immediate context to join others in the service, they see and react to their surroundings together.

Interdependence—Young people who participate in service together must depend on one another for different tasks, and they must learn to rely on one another if they are to accomplish their own task. Some discover new capacities for leadership, while others learn to take a back seat. Some discover unrealized capacities which typical classroom learning doesn't bring forth. And all learn that others have skills and can contribute in significant ways. A major study of experiential education (of which service-learning is a subset) found that 86 percent of participants said the experience increased their sense of responsibility to the group or class.[5]

Enriched Study—Service-learning intentionally reverses the common classroom learning pattern in which students are given information, then asked to go apply it. In service-learning, the process begins with the experience of serving others, which is then followed up with the information they need.

As one of the leaders in service-learning, Dan Conrad, writes, "We begin with real life experiences and aim to build out of these a more general understanding of human beings and their world, and greater competence to act effectively within that world."[6] This approach more closely resembles the way people learn, and thus holds tremendous promise for education in youth-ministry programs.

17

Youth Empowerment and Leadership—Through service-learning, young people recognize their strengths and gain skills to make a difference in the world. They gain an enhanced self-image, a knowledge base of relevant information, skills to accomplish goals, a sense of purpose, and an ability to work with others. By nurturing these qualities, youth service-learning builds a strong leadership base among young people.

New Relations with Teachers and Other Adults—Too often, teenagers are passive recipients in the church. Everything is done for them or to them. We teach them what they "need" to know and tell them what they "should" do. Some are interested and attentive to our efforts. The majority tune us out, passively waiting for something else to come along that strikes their fancy. Service-learning shifts the emphasis—the young people have responsibility, ownership, and leadership. Leaders become facilitators more than presenters of information, and their relationships with young people improve.

On another level, service-learning can transform expectations and perspectives about being involved in a youth group. Veteran youth worker and pastor Dean Feldmeyer notes that teenagers grow up in a consumer culture, and they bring it with them to church. "We're constantly in competition with the consumer culture," Feldmeyer says. "But we really can't compete."

Through service, Feldmeyer believes, a church announces that it may not be able to satisfy all the young people's consumer desires, but it can offer something meaningful. "The goal," he says, "is to help young people begin to see themselves not as consumers of religion and the church, but as practitioners of the faith."

Opportunity for Learning

It's not news that experience can be the best teacher. However, we often forget this truth in our Christian education programs, in which we read about things, talk about things, sing about things, and pray about things, but rarely *do* things—*real* things, not simulations.

If you read the magazines and books, and attend the workshops in youth ministry, you know what we mean. There's a lot of talk about experiential, or active, learning in youth ministry. Book after book is filled with ideas and games and programs and simulations designed to help young people learn through experience.

While there are notable exceptions, particularly in theoretical literature, you'll be hard-pressed to find many youth-ministry resources that hold up direct service—real experience with real issues in the real world—as a vehicle for learning.[7] Some highlight a pyramid of teaching methods, noting that direct experience is the best teacher. But in parentheses beside direct experience, they put "simulations" or "active learning." If they do discuss direct experience in the real world, they focus on camping and rock-climbing and other types of physically challenging experiential education. While all these approaches certainly have a place in the church's ministry and can be steps toward service-learning, it seems that learning through service is conspicuously absent.

The service-learning approach offers that opportunity and challenge to the church. The model builds on the conceptual research of David Kolb, in which he argued that complete learning is a four-part cycle, which begins with concrete experience.[8] Service-learning naturally builds on this model and intentionally includes all the components, as Figure 2 shows.

Figure 2
The Service-Learning Cycle

Service-learning addresses each step of the experiential learning cycle developed by David Kolb. The headings are Kolb's and the narratives illustrate the application to youth work. In parentheses is an example of the way the process builds on itself.

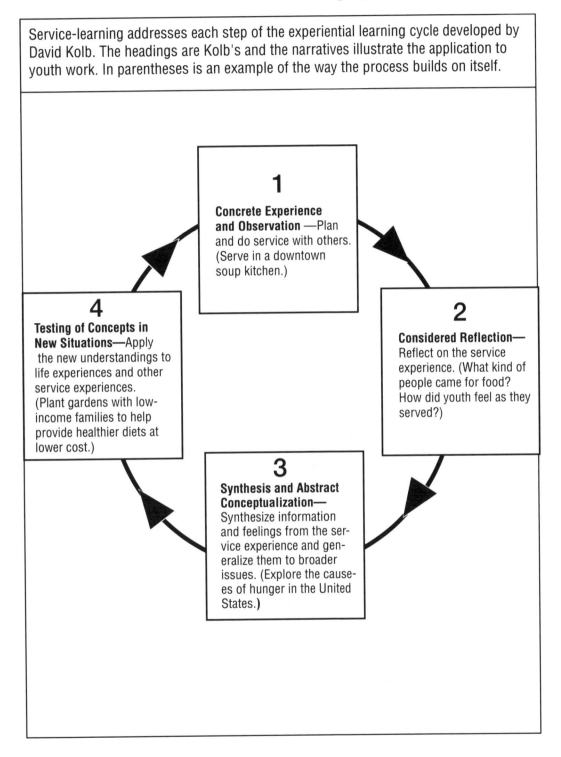

1

Concrete Experience and Observation —Plan and do service with others. (Serve in a downtown soup kitchen.)

2

Considered Reflection— Reflect on the service experience. (What kind of people came for food? How did youth feel as they served?)

3

Synthesis and Abstract Conceptualization— Synthesize information and feelings from the service experience and generalize them to broader issues. (Explore the causes of hunger in the United States.)

4

Testing of Concepts in New Situations—Apply the new understandings to life experiences and other service experiences. (Plant gardens with low-income families to help provide healthier diets at lower cost.)

The service-learning approach has tremendous power for learning. "The power of service as a path to learning is that it places young people in the context in which the learning is real, alive, and has clear consequences for others and for themselves," write service-learning pioneers Dan Conrad and Diane Hedin. "It does not reach everybody, but it reaches a far higher percentage, more deeply, than any other method we have tried."[9]

The same reality translates into our efforts to teach the foundations of the faith, which are more effective and long-lasting when young people learn and practice them *at the same time*, rather than waiting until they have "figured everything out" and try to "put their faith into practice" when they become adults.

The emphasis on learning is one of the major factors that distinguishes service-learning from other community service programs. "Service-learning programs . . . build in structures—pre-service preparation, seminars, group discussions, journals, readings, debriefing, or others—that actively support participants to learn from their service experiences."[10]

Service-learning clearly has potential as a central learning strategy in Christian education. And its particular power comes as it engages Christians in intentional acts of service, then calls them to reflect on that experience and its meaning for their lives.

Impact on the Community

Structured learning is one key difference between service-learning and community service in general. A second difference, according to Jane Kendall, is "reciprocity."

> *Reciprocity* is the exchange of giving and receiving between the "server" and the person or group "being served." All parties in service-learning are learners and help to determine what is to be learned. Both the server and those served teach, and both learn. Such service-learning exchanges avoid the traditionally paternalistic, one-way approach to service, in which one person or group has resources which they share "charitably" or "voluntarily" with a person or group that lacks resources.[11]

When youth groups enter partnership with communities and individuals to provide services, these efforts can have a significant impact on the community and the individuals who receive the service—just as it does on the young people themselves.[12]

Impact on Service Recipients—In *The Workcamp Experience*, John Shaw tells of a group of teenagers who participated in a week-long work camp on a Native American reservation in Montana. The six-member crew was assigned to restore the home of an older man whose wife had died three years earlier, leaving him depressed. "The work crew was assigned a list of tough projects for the week," Shaw writes—"painting inside and out, repairing broken windows and doors, rebuilding the back steps and putting a new roof on the house."

Despite the somewhat daunting task, the young people took it on with vigor, even helping the man clean the house and do the laundry, which had stacked up for three years because he didn't know how to use the washing machine. Shaw finishes the story:

> By the end of the week, the crew members had a new friend they called "Gramps," and he had a huge smile on his face to go along with his rejuvenated house. When I visited the work site, the resident beamed with happiness as he bounced across the room to show me the closets full of freshly washed clothes. And he proudly told me that his new friends had taught him how to use the washer.[13]

When done with respect and sensitivity, service can empower people in need to regain control of their lives. As the above story illustrates, the service not only fixes porches or paints walls, but provides a breakthrough that renews the energy of recipients and gives them new hope. In many cases, the service can provide the needed resources and skills that had prevented individuals from leading quality lives.

Impact on Issues—While young people may have trouble understanding abstract social issues, they can become effective activists when the issues become personalized and concrete.

Barbara A. Lewis tells how her sixth-grade class became environmental activists when students discovered a possible hazardous-waste dump just three blocks from the school. "That old barrel yard?" asked eleven-year-old Maxine when the place was shown on a map of the city. "Kids climb all over those barrels." Quickly, curiosity grew. The students rallied their peers, then began taking action. First the sixth-graders went to officials, who dismissed their concerns, not taking them seriously. So the students went door-to-door, alerting neighbors. But still no action.

When no one seemed to be listening, the students contacted the media. They began reading up on the issues and invited guest speakers. They contacted the Environmental Protection Agency. Then finally, they took their concern to the mayor, a former schoolteacher. He listened, and things started to happen.

The mayor influenced the EPA (which originally had dismissed the students) to issue a report on the hazardous materials at the site. In the end, the site was cleaned up, two new environmental laws were signed, and other improvements were made in the neighborhood. And it all started because those sixth-graders wouldn't give up on an issue that was important to them.[14]

While this story took place in a public school, it illustrates the impact that young people can have on a particular issue or concern. By involving their youth in service and social issues, congregations can tap a valuable resource for the community. As a report from the William T. Grant Commission on Work, Family, and Citizenship argues, "There is virtually no limit to what young people . . . can do, no social need they cannot help meet." The report continues that giving young people opportunities to serve enables them to "become contributors, problem-solvers, and partners with adults in improving their communities and larger society."[15]

Impact on Community Climate—As important as the impact on specific individuals and issues may be, there is a deeper impact when young people are involved in service and action—the impact it can have on a community's climate and values. Leaders in service-learning, James C. Kielsmeier and Rick Jackson, put it this way:

> Our present and future internal security is dependent on a citizenry who are invested in this nation. Citizenship is learned behavior taught through progressive involvement in the community—taught through service at every age and development level.[16]

As youth in a community become active in service, several significant consequences emerge. First, young people will increasingly be viewed by adults as *resources*, rather than as nuisances or problems. And over time, a tradition of youth service could alter community values to the point at which service becomes normative, a social expectation promulgated by both adults and the young. In this way, a community becomes real community, where people share a common vision and watch out for one another. In such a climate, children and teenagers prosper.

Many youth experts now believe that youth welfare could be greatly enhanced if a number of youth-serving sectors (congregations, schools, voluntary organizations like Scouts, Girls, Inc., YMCA, and YWCA) could work together by creating a shared vision

21

and developing a community plan for promoting child and adolescent well-being. It may be that the bridge which unites these sectors is service. Service could become a common bond, a common interest that would lead congregations to be in conversation with schools and voluntary organizations to provide opportunities for sharing training events, information, and resources. Out of this shared experience could come alliances and partnerships that enhance the capacity of a community to meet the needs of all its young.

A Missed Opportunity

Given the potential of service-learning, how much are churches taking advantage of this opportunity? Well, there's good news and there's bad news.

- *The Good News*—The church tends to be the main gateway to service for teenagers. The Independent Sector survey found that 62 percent of teen volunteers learned about their volunteer activities through their religious institution. Next in the list came school (34%), and another voluntary organization (23%).[17] A Gallup Youth Poll found that teenagers who go to church regularly are twice as likely as others to volunteer (31% vs. 16%).[18]

- *The Bad News*—Most young people have had virtually no exposure to service through their congregations. According to the Effective Christian Education study, only 29 percent of congregations emphasize involving young people in service projects in their youth ministries. As a result, more than half the young people have spent five or fewer hours *in their lifetime* "doing projects to help people in my town or city" (64% of 13–15-year-olds and 54% of 16–18-year-olds). Similar percentages of teenagers say they have spent five hours or fewer in their lifetime "learning about or doing something about people who are poor and hungry" (58% of 13–15-year-olds and 53% of 16–18-year-olds).

- *More Good News*—Though young people aren't involved in service much through churches, our research shows that they are somewhat interested in service opportunities. Similarly, a Gallup Poll found that while only 23 percent are involved in church-sponsored charitable activities, 54 percent indicated they would like to be involved. This interest is higher than interest in Sunday school (14%), church group (23%), or church music (18%).[19]

- *More Bad News*—Though 57 percent of congregations in the Effective Christian Education study offer some sort of community-service projects for youth, few have intentionally made the connection between service and learning. Leaders in the service-learning movement know of few congregations that actually have connected to the movement—though they see the opportunity as enormous.

Thus, despite the potential, few congregations appear to be taking full advantage of the opportunity that service-learning presents. Religious educator Donald G. Elmer writes:

Even with the church finally responding to societal issues, religious educators do not seem to adequately know how to equip and enable learners to participate in the ministries of peace and justice. The most religious educators know how to do is to tell learners that they should be concerned.[20]

Beyond Leaf Raking is an attempt to make those connections. It can be read from two perspectives. On the one hand, it attempts to show Christian educators how to take

Figure 3
What Are Your Priorities?

Service-learning has many potential benefits for youth, most of which are outlined in this chapter. Which ones are most important to you? Use this rating sheet to rate their importance: from 5=very important to 1=not important at all. Compare your answers with others involved in planning your youth program (including the young people) until you develop a common understanding of your priorities.

I want to involve young people in service . . .

1. To help them fulfill the biblical call to serve others.	1	2	3	4	5
2. To solidify their commitment to and involvement in the congregation.	1	2	3	4	5
3. To nurture young people's growth in faith.	1	2	3	4	5
4. To promote healthy lifestyles and choices among teenagers.	1	2	3	4	5
5. To develop positive self-esteem, self-confidence, and social skills.	1	2	3	4	5
6. To teach young people new skills and perspectives.	1	2	3	4	5
7. To nurture a lifelong commitment to service and justice involvement.	1	2	3	4	5
8. To build a stronger sense of community in the youth group.	1	2	3	4	5
9. To have an impact on individual people who are served by the program.	1	2	3	4	5
10. To help them have an impact on critical issues facing our community, nation, and world.	1	2	3	4	5
11. To improve the quality and climate of our community.	1	2	3	4	5
12. To develop youth ownership and leadership in youth ministry.	1	2	3	4	5
13. To help the congregation and community se youth as vital resources.	1	2	3	4	5
Other reason:	1	2	3	4	5
Other reason:	1	2	3	4	5

advantage of the powerful educational opportunities offered by service. Thus it challenges youth workers to rethink the way they educate young people about the faith.

On the other hand, *Beyond Leaf Raking* is for people who have become frustrated by their inability to involve youth in meaningful service and justice activities—people who aren't content that young people place low priority on these issues. This book seeks to infuse service and justice with the understanding that these activities are catalysts for learning, that they broaden perspectives in ways that nurture lifelong commitment to social issues and human needs.

It might be said that our goal is to offer congregations a new way of thinking about the relationship between service and education. Indeed, it may be a new way of thinking about youth ministry, since young people's involvement in the church and their education in the faith take place through active application of their faith to the issues and needs of the day.

It is our hope that this book will stimulate congregations to rediscover the power of service to reinvigorate youth ministry and bring the gospel to a world eager for a message of hope and healing.

2 THE IMPACT OF SERVICE-LEARNING

It's not too unusual for a church to run an after-school program for inner-city children. But it is unusual when that program is coordinated and directed by a youth group, as it is at Ginghamsburg United Methodist Church in Tipp City, Ohio. Since 1990, one hundred teens in the youth group have been running the program, which consists of three "clubhouses" in Dayton, which serve fifty children, four days a week.

The young people's service doesn't stop with the clubhouses, however. The group plans, prepares, and serves a Thanksgiving dinner for people in the community, helps insulate homes for low-income families, builds homes in Appalachia each summer, and undertakes a range of other service projects.[1]

How did this youth group get so involved in serving others? It began in the early 1980s, when Mike Nygren became the youth pastor. He had a vision of one day having his youth group spend a day each month in a service project. Then a fourteen-year-old girl said that she wanted to do something in an inner-city neighborhood. Her sense of calling to ministry evolved into the clubhouse program.

Today, service is at the core of the youth program, which draws about two hundred youths a week. "Our reputation is that we're serious about what we do," Nygren says. "It becomes a way of life."

What's more, service has become the catalyst for growth in faith and commitment. Unlike most youth programs, the Ginghamsburg group keeps students active all the way through high school. Less than 5 percent of the young people who become involved in seventh grade leave the program before graduation, Nygren says. "They're maturing in their faith through their work." As a result, the church has seen a disproportionate number of group members choose life vocations dedicated to ministry, mission, and service.

The Ginghamsburg church story exemplifies what can happen to a youth ministry when service becomes central to the program. It also highlights some of the potential benefits of involvement for the young people, the youth group, and ultimately, the whole community. And the church's experience parallels much of what has been learned about the potential benefit—and possible outcomes—of youth service.

Bonding Youth to the Church

In spite of widespread perceptions that the emphasizing of service may drive young people away from church, there is evidence that the opposite may be true, with young people's commitment to the church increasing with their level of service involvement.

In 1990, Search Institute released Effective Christian Education, a national study of 560 congregations in six denominations.[2] In that study, we asked 3,000 churchgoing 7th-through 12th-graders whether they strongly agreed with the statement, "The church I attend matters a great deal to me."

Among young people who had given no time in service through their congregation in their lifetime, only 20 percent strongly agreed with that statement. But the percentage doubled to 43 percent among those who had spent 40 or more hours in service *in their lifetime* through the congregation (see Figure 4).

Figure 4
Service Increases Youths' Bond to the Church

Number of hours spent in church programs aimed at "helping people in my town or city" in lifetime	Churched youth who strongly agree that their church means a great deal to them	Churched youth who say there is an "excellent chance" they will be involved in church when they are . . .		Churched youth who say it is "very important" to them to belong to a church
		21 years old	**40 years old**	
0 hours	20%	14%	17%	24%
1-2 hours	24%	15%	19%	28%
3-5 hours	25%	19%	25%	28%
6-10 hours	23%	20%	28%	32%
11-20 hours	32%	24%	32%	40%
21-40 hours	39%	28%	38%	41%
More than 40 hours	43%	40%	39%	45%
Average of all	30%	25%	34%	34%

The more time youth gives in service to the community through the congregation, the greater the loyalty and bonding to the church, according to Search Institute research. This chart shows young people's responses to several issues, based on their involvement in service through the congregation.

Similar patterns emerged when young people indicated the likelihood that they would be active in church as adults. The percentage more than doubled for their anticipated involvement both at age 21 and at age 40. And finally, young people who were most active in service through their congregations were almost twice as likely to say that "it is very important to me to belong to a church," when compared to those who had been involved in no service.

No one would argue that having just 40 percent of its youth loyal to the congregation is an ideal situation. But when compared to the overall averages for churchgoing young people, it suggests that service could be an important vehicle for nurturing loyalty. As young people experience meaningful service and discover its impact on their faith and life, they become more loyal to the organization that provided the opportunity. Furthermore, bonds among those who serve side-by-side also keep young people active because of their shared experience and the relationships that form through the service.

Nurturing Growth in Faith

Not only does service involvement appear to nurture stronger ties to the congregation, but it is a powerful factor in nurturing faith. According to Ridge Burns and Noel Becchetti:

In our nearly thirty years of combined youth ministry experience, we've found nothing brings kids face-to-face with Jesus like mission and service. There is something about putting the challenge to "offer your bodies as living sacrifices, holy and pleasing to God" (Rom. 12:1) into practice that changes lives, pure and simple.[3]

Search Institute research finds a similar impact of service involvement on the nurturing of faith. At the heart of the Effective Christian Education study was a scale designed to assess faith maturity and growth in faith. In that framework, faith maturity was defined as having two dimensions: a life-transforming relationship with a loving God, and a consistent devotion to serving others.[4]

In the survey, we asked adults to recall their experiences in church as children and youth. We found that those who were higher in faith maturity were more likely to have been involved in service projects as children and teenagers. In fact, their involvement in service was a better predictor of their faith maturity as adults than were their memories of participation in Sunday school, Bible study, or worship services.[5]

We see a similarly powerful relationship between service and faith when young people talk about their growth in faith in the past two or three years. Young people are more likely to report growth in faith if . . .

. . . their congregation does a good job of getting them involved in "helping to improve the lives of people who are poor or hungry";
. . . their congregation does a good job of getting them involved in "helping people in your town or city";
. . . they have spent more time in their lifetime learning about and doing something through the church for people who are poor or hungry;
. . . they have spent more time in their lifetime in helping projects through the church.[6]

One reason for this positive impact on faith maturity may be that service-learning incorporates many of the elements of an effective Christian education program and recognizes the power of experience as a teacher. The Search Institute study identified a range of factors that are key to developing a Christian education program that will nurture faith in teenagers. Many of those factors are hallmarks of the service-learning model. Indeed, the report stated, "The importance of educational process, in tandem with educational content, suggests that the effective program not only teaches in the classical sense of transmitting insight and knowledge, but also allows insights to emerge from the crucible of experience."[7]

All the following aspects of a Christian education program for youth which nurtures growth in faith—as measured in the Effective Christian Education study—are integral to a service-learning approach:

—Emphasizes intergenerational contact;
—Uses life experience as occasion for spiritual insight;
—Creates a sense of community in which people help one another develop faith and values;
—Encourages independent thinking and questioning;
—Involves youth in service projects;
—Emphasizes values and moral decision-making;
—Emphasizes responsibility for poverty and hunger;
—Teaches the Bible and core theological concepts (which service-learning does through preparation and debriefing);
—Teaches youth how to be friends and make friends;
—Helps youth develop concern for other people.

Thus, many of the keys to an effective Christian education program are intrinsic in a well-designed service-learning approach. By making service a cornerstone of our educational programs, we have opportunities to nurture faith in effective ways. Service-learning starts with the power of experience in the learning process. The "doing" is then processed in ways that shape the "feeling" and "thinking."

Promoting a Healthy Life-style

Most congregations recognize that youth ministry involves more than a narrow definition of "spiritual" issues. They see the need for congregations to play a role in promoting healthy choices by teenagers so that they grow up healthy and well-rounded. Like others in our society, churches worry about the negative behaviors and choices made by many teenagers. Thus they intentionally include current issues—alcohol and other drugs, sexuality, movies, dating, and so on—in their youth programming.

While it may not explicitly address these issues, young people who are involved in service are less likely to engage in risky behaviors. Another Search Institute study, *The Troubled Journey*, examined the lives of 47,000 young people in 6th- through 12th-grades in public schools across the United States. It was found that those who serve just one hour or more a week are less likely to be involved in at-risk behaviors than those who are not active in serving others. Out of the 20 at-risk behaviors measured, males who served averaged 2.0 at-risk behaviors, compared to 3.4 for males who spent no time serving. Females who served averaged 2.2 indicators, compared to 2.9 for females who did not serve.[8]

While other factors play a role in the differences between servers and nonservers, comparing specific at-risk behaviors suggests some areas where being involved in service can have a positive impact, since servers are about half as likely to be involved as nonservers in a variety of at-risk behaviors. For example, 14 percent of nonservers frequently use alcohol, but only 7 percent of frequent servers do. Similar differences occur in areas of binge drinking (30% of nonservers vs. 18% of servers), problem drug use (18% of nonservers vs. 9% of servers), daily cigarette use (18% of nonservers vs. 9% of servers), vandalism (13% of nonservers versus 7% of servers), and skipping school (13% of nonservers vs. 7% of servers).

Why does service involvement have a deterring impact on negative behaviors? *The Troubled Journey* suggests a number of possibilities. The study identified 30 assets in young people's lives that reduce at-risk involvement. Several of these are integral to service:

—Service projects provide positive, structured activities for youth. Young people who are involved in these kinds of positive activities are less likely to be involved in negative behaviors.
—Service nourishes caring values as young people relate to and empathize with others. And people who care about others are less likely to be involved in negative behaviors.
—Service also provides a positive climate where young people are influenced positively by their peers, parents, and other adults. This positive influence counterbalances negative influences that might lead to poor choices.
—Young people who have strong relationships with adults other than their parents are less likely to be involved in at-risk behaviors. Thus, service projects that bring youth into contact with all ages could have a deterring effect.

Because service appears to promote healthy life-styles and discourage negative choices, many people believe it is an important resource for addressing some of the pressing youth issues of the day, including violence, substance abuse, school dropouts, and teenage pregnancy.

In addition to its apparent deterring impact on negative behaviors, service involvement appears to nurture important life skills and values in young people. Perhaps the most systematic evaluation of the impact of experiential education (of which service-learning is a significant subset) was the National Assessment of Experiential Education undertaken by Dan Conrad and Diane Hedin, which evaluated 27 experiential programs with 4,000 students.[9] Figure 5 shows what those students said they gained from the programs. Further analysis by the researchers indicated impact in the following areas:

Psychological Development—While some research suggests that traditional classroom learning can sometimes lower self-esteem, responsibility, and interest in learning, experiential education appears to have the opposite effect. Conrad and Hedin found that students involved in experiential learning gain in both moral reasoning and self-esteem.

Social Development—Through service-learning, young people develop new social skills as well as a stronger sense of duty or responsibility for social welfare. Young people involved in the programs showed greater motivation to take action, rather than changed attitudes.[10] In addition, young people in these programs developed more positive attitudes toward adults and other teens.

Intellectual Development—Three-fourths of the students in the experiential-learning programs reported learning "more" or "much more" than in traditional education settings. The most effective programs in this area were those that included intentional opportunities for reflection and processing on the experience, and those that were longer (at least 12 weeks) and more intense.[11]

The impact may not seem dramatic, but changes do occur—sometimes in almost humorous ways. Karen McKinney tells about what would happen after the teenagers returned from the summer Servant Leadership Project at Zion Baptist Church: "A lot of the parents would call me to say, 'She didn't ask for clothes!'" She also remembers one young person who gave up fast food. These changes may not seem profound, she notes, but they indicate that the young people's values were challenged and reshaped by their service and exposure to issues and concerns in the world.

Researchers Dan Conrad and Diane Hedin surveyed 4,000 students who participated in experiential-education programs (of which service-learning is a subset). Here are the percentages of students who agreed or strongly agreed that each item was something they learned from their experience.[12]

Figure 5
What Youth Gain from Service-Learning

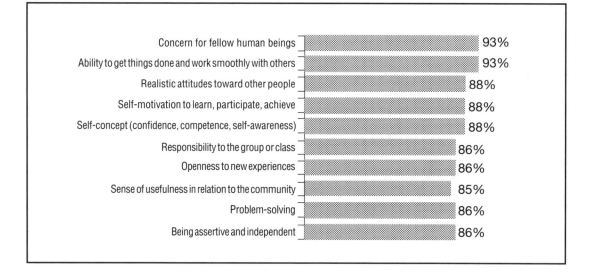

Teaching Life Skills

When we think of community service, too often we think of those who have-it-all-together reaching out to the everything-fell-apart. Because of its emphasis on reciprocity (both servant and recipient benefiting), service-learning breaks down these preconceptions and limitations.

In fact, one of the most hopeful and encouraging benefits of service-learning is its potential for high-risk youth who have few options in life because of where they live. These are the marginalized young people who are particularly at risk, for example, of dropping out of school, becoming sexually active, or being involved in gangs or drugs.

For these youth, service-learning can offer the opportunity not only to develop a sense of personal responsibility and efficacy, but to learn skills that are necessary for a productive adulthood. As a Children's Defense Fund report argues, "The experience gained through service can make a lasting difference, giving young people a sense of purpose and a reason to remain in school, strive to learn, and avoid too-early pregnancy."[13]

Urban congregations are most likely to confront the need to teach such life skills (though suburban and rural congregations will be increasingly challenged to address these issues). Many of their young people have few opportunities to learn new skills, see positive role models, and be motivated or challenged to contribute to the community. And, as Anne Lewis comments, "Service opportunities stimulate skills specifically useful for future employment—skills which many urban youth do not see modeled in their neighborhoods—punctuality and reliability, responsibility for task completion, getting along with others, and good grooming."[14]

At the same time, it can sometimes be difficult to challenge urban youth to see the value of community service. "Many urban youth feel alienated and hostile toward their community and toward institutions in particular," Lewis continues. "Thus, community service can become equated with institutions of which they disapprove and be difficult to 'sell' as something worthwhile."[15]

Despite these obstacles, the potential for community service—among all youth—is strong. By connecting them to their communities while teaching them valuable life skills, congregations can be an important resource in reclaiming youth. Society has been too quick to dismiss the adolescent generation or to see youth as a problem to be controlled. Through service-learning, youth can become a valuable contributor to rebuilding society.

Developing a Lifelong Service Ethic

Getting young people involved in service has a long-term payoff. Those early service experiences have staying power and influence well into adulthood. One needs only listen to activists as they tell their experiences as children and youth to recognize the impact of those early experiences. Hillary Rodham Clinton, for example, credits much of her concern for low-income families and their children to her visits to inner-city Chicago with her church youth group. Many on the mission field and in service vocations have similar stories.

Developmental theorists suggest that experiences during adolescence have a powerful shaping force on lifelong values and sense of purpose. Robert Coles, for example, argues that youthful experiences shape the "moral growth" of adulthood. One's ideals and values are shaped, he says, by early encounters with others and by cross-cultural experiences.[16]

31

Data from the Effective Christian Education study underscore the significance of service early in life. Using survey responses from adults, we examined the frequency with which adults were involved in serving others and working for justice, depending upon their involvement in various activities when young. We determined that the best predictors of adult involvement were their experiences in helping projects as children (ages 5–12) and adolescents (ages 13–18). Each of these experiences discriminates between inactive and active service-givers better than childhood involvement in worship or Christian education.

Similarly, the best predictor of involvement in justice issues as adults was their involvement in justice issues as a teenager. (Among adults who are inactive in justice issues, only 10 percent participated in justice projects as teens; among justice-active adults, 35 percent did so.) Furthermore, note that adults who are active in social justice issues tend to have participated in service projects as a child and/or teenager. The inference is that early experience with giving has long-term effects, setting a pattern that can carry over into adulthood.

This lifelong impact of service involvement points to the potential powerful influence of a youth ministry—not only for the present moment, but on life choices, including vocation and career. In *Growing Up in America,* Anthony Campolo argues that one of the problems facing today's generation of young people is that they have become apathetic; they have no sense of purpose:

> We must inspire young people to greatness. By helping young people see themselves as agents of God's revolution, commissioned to a vocation of ultimate importance, we can provide them with a sense of calling that generates unparalleled enthusiasm for life.[17]

Youth workers see this impact in many ways. Several whom we talked with told of high-school seniors who focused their college-application essays around a particular service experience. One year, Beverly Crowe Tipton took her youth group, from Seventh and James Baptist Church in Waco, Texas, to work with Native Americans in Oklahoma. The process included regular discussions about the struggles and injustices that native people face. A year later, one of the students applied to a university with a long-term goal of working in legal affairs, as an advocate for Native Americans.

Reshaping the Role of Adult Leaders

If your congregation takes seriously the place of service-learning in your youth-education program, it will have a major impact on the role of teachers and youth workers, in both their methods and their experiences. While these shifts may be difficult for some and require training, they include several positive benefits for teachers. Those that follow here have been adapted for youth ministry from the framework of Faye Caskey.

Service-learning broadens the Christian-education curriculum and reverses the traditional educational method. Whereas traditional learning begins with classroom presentation and (ideally) moves to application, service-learning moves in the other direction, beginning with real-life experiences, then generalizing from those experiences to create understanding.

Teachers and youth workers take new roles as mentors and guides, as students take more responsibility for their own learning. The leader is no longer responsible for the whole content of learning. Each person brings experience and insight. As Caskey writes, "The teacher becomes the midwife of accurate knowledge and personal meaning." This does not mean that teachers no longer need skills or have responsibility; rather, it means that teachers need different skills and fulfill other responsibilities, to ensure that the learning is responsible and effective.

Service-learning nurtures new, positive relationships between adults and youth. As young people take responsibility for their own learning, and adult workers take new roles as mentors and guides, relationships between adults and youth change. Adults begin to see youth as competent and insightful, and youth no longer perceives that adults "think they have all the answers."

Carol Davis Younger, a youth worker in Kansas, recalls taking an intergenerational group on a mission trip to work with Native American children. In the evenings, the group led urban children in various activities and learning. In this case, the chair of the congregation's board of deacons was paired with the youngest girl in the group.

The first night, the pair had a terrible time managing the children they had been assigned to for the week. The deacon decided they weren't going to get anywhere in trying to teach anything, so he changed the plan: They would just have fun together.

But the girl wasn't ready to give up, and she worked out some ways to get the children more interested and involved. The deacon wasn't convinced, but they tried her plan. And it worked—in more ways than one. In this case, a young person stretched an adult to grow. "It kind of showed [the deacon] that a young person could get him more involved," Younger explains.

Service-learning reshapes the way we measure the effectiveness of our teaching. While testing doesn't hold a central place in most youth programs, youth workers do have expectations about what young people need to learn. Service-learning challenges youth programs to consider how well the young people have incorporated a living faith into their daily lives, as opposed to how many theological concepts they have memorized. (It should be noted that young people certainly can learn theological concepts through service-learning, but that isn't the focus.)

Service-learning allows adults to act on their faith in the community. Most people who teach in Christian-education programs say they learn more than they teach. This same principle is even more true in service-learning. As adults study and work side-by-side with teenagers, they too apply their faith, examine their lives, and apply their faith to issues in the world. And because they aren't the sole source of information for learning, they often gain as much knowledge from the reflection on service as the young people do.[18]

A Portrait of Youth Who Serve

What kinds of young people are predisposed to helping others? The answer to this question has some important implications for the design of service projects. According to Search Institute research on 47,000 students in public schools, girls are more likely than boys to think that it is important to serve and reach out to others. For both boys and girls, the value declines throughout high school.[19]

Precisely the same pattern holds for actual helping behavior. Higher percentages of girls than boys devote time to "helping people who are poor, hungry, sick, or unable to care for themselves." This difference occurs for every grade between 6 and 12.

Thus, there is a steady decline in prosocial values and in helping behavior across the adolescent years. This decline occurs for both boys and girls, but across time, the gap between boys and girls widens. There are three important lessons here:

—Girls are more likely to serve than boys.
—Service declines dramatically across the adolescent years for both boys and girls.
—The gender gap widens between grades 6 and 12.

What does all this mean for constructing effective congregational service projects? First, we can see the importance of the task. Today's youth lives in a society with powerful and intoxicating messages about individualism and paying attention to "me." During the formative adolescent years, there occurs a clear erosion of what had been strong prosocial instincts evident in late childhood (grade 6).

The numbers are testimony to our society's success, unintended as it may be, in socializing the young away from the kind of caring and compassionate commitments so necessary to the long-term well-being of society and, we might add, to the well-being of individual lives. It becomes important, then, to rally congregational energy to help inhibit this national slide away from caring. And there is no better time to intervene than in the formative period of adolescence.

We also can see in these numbers the strong message that middle-school students (grades 6 and 7, particularly) possess strong prosocial instincts. A challenge to congregations is to maintaining this energy by offering strong service opportunities for young adolescents. Indeed, grade 5—at about ages 10-11—may be the best time to begin a strong service program. Youth involved in effective service-learning between grades 5 and 7 will be less likely to experience an erosion in service values and behavior, because such experiences will cement, solidify, and ground the value of giving within one's emerging self-concept. Ultimately, the ideal is to make service a programming priority in grade 5 and continue this emphasis all the way through the adolescent years.

And then there is the gender difference. Perhaps this is due to differences in socialization. We expect girls to be helpers, and we expect (and permit) "boys to be boys." Congregations need to be sensitive to this pattern, working diligently and consciously to encourage boys to take an interest in the business of service. It can be done, particularly when boys are embedded in a congregational environment where it is normative, expected, and valued for males to serve. Nothing would be more powerful here than surrounding young boys with service-oriented adult male role models.

Other Factors That Promote Service

While age and gender are key issues in the development of prosocial youth, other factors also matter. A great deal of social-science research attests to six distinguishing characteristics of teenagers who maintain a commitment to service:
1. Empathy—have the ability to understand and care about the feelings of others.
2. Peer group—are a part of a network of friends that values helping.
3. Adult role models—observe adults participating in service.
4. Family environment—are part of a warm and nurturing family.
5. Family helping projects—are in a family where parents and children together engage in projects to help others. This is doubly powerful when parents help children see service as an expression of religious faith.
6. Horizontal faith—develop a religious faith that includes dimensions that are both vertical (establishing a close relationship to a loving God) and horizontal (knowing and believing that mature faith includes a commitment to service).

Each of these pro-helping factors can be addressed or encouraged by congregations in their overall attempt to teach service. The development of a service orientation requires more than just service programs done with the young. There is also a place for family education, for theological education, and for taking advantage of a congregation's intergenerational capacity, in which adult role models develop meaningful relationships with children and teenagers. Thus, the remainder of this book describes, in practical terms, how congregations can build youth programs that nurture a life-style of service, through which young people's faith and commitment grow.

3 TEN QUESTIONS FOR SHAPING YOUR PROGRAM

You think service-learning is a good idea. You've had enough experience to know its potential, and you can see the benefits it would have for your youth group. Yet the possibilities seem so endless. Where do you start? How do you decide what kinds of projects to do?

This chapter is built around ten questions that are foundational for shaping your approach to service-learning. As you answer these questions and make these choices, your program will begin to take shape.

1. What Do We Hope to Learn?

As we think about service-learning, an early question should be, What do we hope young people will learn? What specific skills or values or issues do we hope to evoke through the hands-on service?

Some possible goals are relatively obvious outcomes of service-learning. Your goal may be straightforward: To help young people learn the life-style of Christian service. Or it may be more complex: To help young people understand the economic and social systems that perpetuate injustice in our world. Either goal can be addressed through service-learning, but you are likely to choose different activities—and you certainly would surround those activities with different types of research, reading, and discussion.

Other goals may be less obvious, but have just as much potential. These might involve . . .

. . . learning theological concepts (forgiveness, grace, redemption, baptism)
. . . learning about social issues (politics, environment, human rights, hunger)
. . . learning Christian responsibility (evangelism, life-style, outreach, activism)
. . . developing life skills (decision-making, responsibility, friendship)
. . . nurturing healthy life-styles (drug-free, sexual responsibility)
. . . enhancing personal attitudes (self-esteem, empowerment, view of future).

Each of these (and other) goals can be designed into a service-learning project through careful selection and reflective processing of experience. Chapter 4 focuses on how to design a service-learning project, and chapter 7 focuses on how to debrief and reflect on service.

While establishing some learning objectives is important for planning, the challenge (and opportunity) of service-learning is that you cannot fully anticipate what young people will learn. They may not see the things you were sure they would see, and something may happen that introduces a completely unexpected "teachable moment." As Dean Feldmeyer, a pastor in Ohio, puts it, "It's helpful to have educational goals in mind, but you have to be open to the opportunities that just happen."

Feldmeyer tells about an experience at a work camp with his youth group. One day halfway through the camp, rain started to pour. As usual, the group ate lunch together, waiting for the rain to stop. Not long after they had finished, the home owner came out and invited them in to share lunch with her.

A bit awkwardly, the group accepted and went inside to a table laid with everything the woman had: roast groundhog, boiled chicken, cornbread, wild raspberries, unmatched silverware, ice water from jelly jars, no napkins. Most of the suburban teens had never eaten anything like what was before them. "They're still talking about it!" Feldmeyer says.

No one could have planned that lunch. But it became a key learning experience for the trip as the group later talked about it. They discussed hospitality. They decided that a person's financial state doesn't determine whether that person can be a servant. And they talked about how that woman had not just invited them to a meal, but had invited them into her life and shared with them all she had.

The scriptural ties soon emerged. Feldmeyer says the group began discussing the true meaning of communion. They looked at the stories of banquets in scripture. And they talked about how it feels to have your feet washed. None of that was included in the learning objectives for that work camp, but it all became part of the rich learning those young people took home.

2. What Is the Church's Tradition?

A youth ministry is inevitably a reflection of the congregation's culture and climate. Most often, the things that are strong in a congregation will be strong in the youth ministry. And unless the congregation has a commitment to service, it will be difficult to persuade it to support such a commitment in the youth ministry.

If the Effective Christian Education study of mainline Protestants is any indication, one of the early challenges a service-learning effort will face is a lack of a strong foundation in the congregation. Only half of all adults say their congregations emphasize reaching out to the poor and hungry, and just 40 percent say that it emphasizes "involving members in helping people in their own town or city." And when the focus moves to advocacy, just 12 percent say their congregations emphasize getting members to work for social justice and peace.

If a congregation does have a strong commitment to service and advocacy, it's natural for the youth program to build on that heritage. Other congregations, though, will have other ideas. For some, service may be focused in women's circles, or it may rely on the energy and dedication of a handful of stalwarts. Some churches may focus their energy on creating a close-knit group. It may be difficult for them to imagine—much less support—emphasizing service-learning in the youth ministry.

While your congregation may not be an activist congregation, it probably has some kind of tradition of service and community involvement. As Carl S. Dudley comments:

> Churches carry a corporate consciousness that provides both delight and frustration to all who try to lead them. It is affirming to know that congregations are more than collections of individuals—they select and socialize their members into perceptions and commitments that are not easily changed. On the other hand, leaders who want to precipitate change are frustrated unless they begin with the church as it is, and build upon the continuities of the past.[1]

Instead of trying to overcome that history, use it as a foundation for your service-learning efforts. For several years, Dudley and the Center for Church and Community Ministries in Chicago have been involved in working with typical Midwest congregations to help them develop social-ministry programs. Researchers identified five congregational images that shape their social ministry:[2]

Prophet churches fit the pattern of highly visible congregations in social ministry. "They turn every issue into a campaign, every crisis into a larger cause," Carl Dudley and Sally Johnson write. They march on the front lines of social causes, raising issues that others might let slide. However, these congregations aren't necessarily the most liberal. In fact, they tend to be theologically moderate or evangelical, though they hold liberal views on social issues.

As a rule, these churches are pioneers that clear the way for others—and for denominations to become involved in controversial issues. "Admirers are tempted to make them the normative model for congregational social ministry. Yet the majority of American Christian congregations build on other identities to generate effective social ministries."[3]

Survivor churches don't seem like good candidates for social ministry. They are "reactive, and always on the verge of being overwhelmed by emergencies." But survivor churches can effectively respond to crises. "They may be reacting with their backs to the wall, but it works," Dudley and Johnson state. "These are activist congregations, second only to crusaders in their corporate commitment to respond to social problems."[4]

These churches find their identity in their survival and persistence, which become motivating forces for helping others in crisis. Indeed, because of their own struggles, these survivors can cope where other congregational styles might collapse.

Pillar churches support and undergird the community with resources and status. When they become involved in social and public issues, they do it out of a sense of civic duty. They tend to study issues longer and, to some, seem slow to act. When mobilized, though, "these churches can have a powerful impact."[5] Their methodical, in-depth study often leads them to develop more comprehensive strategies than other congregations, enabling them to meet multifaceted needs when they address the problem.

Though the pillar churches in Dudley and Johnson's study tend to be liberal on theological issues, they are more conservative on social issues. But the pillars can legitimate change where others might ignore it. And when they do become involved, they often quickly move to advocacy due to their prominence in the community.

Pilgrim churches, which often have an ethnic makeup, are rooted in their people and their heritage, not a place. Ministries generally happen through cultural networks. These churches have a deep sense of responsibility to society's outcasts.

Pilgrim churches might not think of themselves as activists, yet they are among the most active in caring for "our people" and, in time, those beyond themselves. They often focus their ministry priorities on long-term improvements in the lives of others. They tend to sponsor, for example, educational efforts such as job training, English classes, parenting skills, and other life skills. And, due to their history, they tend to be conscious of systemic and global issues, which quickly push them into advocacy roles.

Servant churches focus their social ministries on quiet care for individuals who otherwise might be lost in larger social agendas. Theirs is a pastoral, personal ministry. They are not motivated by causes, but faithfully help people.

As might be expected, these congregations tend to be socially conservative and theologically moderate. For them, caring for others is a natural part of their faith. As a result, they effectively help individuals in need to "get back on their feet" by doing home repairs, helping with insurance paperwork or with finding a job.

Each of these images opens up possibilities for a youth program that seeks to become involved in service. For example, a youth group in a "survivor" church might choose to participate in a hurricane-relief effort. A group in a servant church might set up a regular schedule of visiting shut-ins. Youth in a pilgrim church might offer tutoring to recent immigrants (both children and adults) who are learning English. Or in a pillar church, they might undertake a project to document some environmental issues the community needs to address.

Support from the congregation is vital to the long-term success of your service-learning emphasis. Unless the adults understand your goals and methods, you may hear statements such as, "Our kids are always doing stuff—why aren't they ever doing Bible study like we used to?" or "I don't understand why we have to contribute so much to send youth to Appalachia when there's plenty to do around here," or "We need to take care of our own instead of always focusing on others."

In reality, though, most congregations will be extremely supportive of an effective service-learning effort. Here are some principles to follow that can help to ensure the support.

Build on your congregation's heritage. Your youth program will be more effective if it builds on your congregation's image instead of trying to overcome it. To discover and build on that heritage, Dudley suggests four basic steps:[6]

- Identify your biblical foundations. "The congregation's biblical faith gives us a window that looks two ways," Dudley writes. "For the church, Scripture is a way to see the world; for identity, Scripture is a way to see the church."
- Find sources in your church heritage. To undergird your efforts, look to the statements of faith, creeds, official pronouncements, stories of saints (official and otherwise), and other aspects of the faith story.
- Build on your congregation's history. Instead of saying, "We're going to do something radically new. You've never seen anything like it," try, "Our congregation has a long history of caring for people in crisis. Our young people are going to connect to this part of our story through a new program that will focus on addressing the needs of the homeless in our community."
- Analyze your strengths and limitations through a survey. Learn about the values and commitments of members. It would be valuable to obtain this information from both the congregation and the youth group.[7]

In these cases, it may take more energy and convincing to involve youth in service-learning, but it is certainly an achievable goal. Here are suggestions that may help to "sell" service-learning to the congregation.

Create a climate for service. Recent research reveals that service programs have their strongest and most sustained impact on youth when they are embedded in a particular kind of congregational milieu.[8] Such an environment has five features: (1) Youth experiences the congregation as a warm and friendly place, in which adults and other young people are open, inviting, and expressive of their support and concern for one another; (2) youth experiences care directly, as when adults and/or peers inquire about school or family, or provide assistance when help is needed; (3) the congregation seeks to integrate young people into the life of the congregation rather than segregating them—that is, congregations take advantage of their intergenerational potential, connecting youth to adults in meaningful ways; (4) the congregation treats service as normative, as something expected and celebrated by those who seek to be faithful; and (5) the congregation nurtures service values throughout its Christian-education program, helping children, teenagers, and adults understand the human and social conditions, both locally and globally, which define the need for service, and providing encouragement and practical suggestions for ways meaningful service can be given.

In creating the kind of congregational climate that will support and encourage service, the following suggestions may be helpful:

- Find ways for youth and adults to be together—for socializing, for fun and recreation, for learning, worship, and study.
- Provide educational events to help youth and adults learn how to show care and concern in interpersonal relationships. Peer counseling training is one good vehicle.
- During worship and in Christian-education programming, hold up and celebrate the importance of service.
- Provide intergenerational events to hear from people—both inside and outside the congregation—who can articulate how faith has led them to serve.

- Begin a mentoring program within the congregation, connecting each child and/or teenager to a caring adult. This provides a wonderful opportunity for building a sustained relationship that could include working together on a food shelf, visiting people in need, or another example of caring.
- Place symbols of caring (posters, banners, announcements) in strategic places where people are likely to see them.

Don't shoot too high. Your dream might be to have a youth ministry that revolves around service. But you're unlikely to gain support for the program if the heart of the current youth program is a Sunday-night recreation and Bible-study time or a traditional Sunday school. In these cases, it might be most workable to begin with small service-learning experiences during the traditional time commitment. Then, over time, as the success grows, you'll discover less resistance to your more comprehensive ideas and plans.

Build congregational investment in the program. One of the problems some have encountered in developing a youth-service program is that the adults in the congregation don't really take it seriously. "Parents and the church don't always see this kind of ministry as being life-changing, but 'sweet'," explains Dave Carver of Twelve Corners Presbyterian Church in Rochester, New York. When the group returns from a service project, "People want to pat them on the back for being nice. And all these heads nod in approval."

In reality, Carver contends, these adults fail to recognize the life-changing experiences that young people have. He blames this on "the failure of the institution to recognize the radical nature of service."

Carver tries to address this issue by helping the congregation understand and support what's really happening with the youth. On the Sunday before a mission trip, the church bulletin includes sentences from work campers that tell what they are looking forward to and what they want prayers for. As Carver puts it, "If you've been praying for Junior all week, you'll probably ask him about the experience when he gets home."

Carver also finds ways to get adults and youth together to talk about the service experiences. As a fund-raiser for mission trips, the youth group lets people "invest" in the trip by buying stock. One of the "dividends" for people who buy stock in the trip is that one of the teenagers goes to visit with the family before the trip. The teenagers talk about the trip—what excites them, what worries them, what fears they have. When adults hear the teenagers speak out of true commitment, they become more supportive and less condescending about the possibilities of youth service.

Plug into congregational programs. Your congregation probably provides financial support to a variety of ministries locally, nationally, and internationally. In fact, an Independent Sector survey found that 87 percent of congregations support human-service activites, 79 percent support international programs, 70 percent support social-action programs, and 68 percent support health-care programs.[9] By having the youth group volunteer for some of these programs, you give the congregation an opportunity to have a direct connection with the programs it funds. Furthermore, it is an effective way to ensure that programs you choose already have support within the congregation.

Help teens talk about their service. One of the problems that can occur when young people become active in service is that they develop superiority complexes. If they spend a week on a work camp, they sometimes have difficulty accepting that the people back home haven't been experiencing the same intense experiences. This can build walls that make it difficult for teens to internalize and talk about their experiences without turning people off.

This is one reason Carver tries to include both youth and adults in local service projects. As teenagers work side by side with adults, Carver prompts them to tell about their experiences in the longer mission trips. In this way, adults who might want to go on a work camp, but can't, at least can be inspired and challenged by teenagers who are more involved.

Integrate youth into the congregation's leadership. Young people's service-learning experiences will be valuable leadership-training grounds, as they grow and mature through service. As they develop these skills, they should be encouraged to use their gifts within the congregation as well. They may find church committees or task forces that are addressing the things they are concerned about. Or they may want to lead activities or teach classes in the church. In whatever ways they show their leadership skills, they enhance the congregation's perception of the youth program.

Carver tells about one group member who became a deacon during his senior year in high school. And while having youth in leadership isn't a novel idea, Carver says, "What pleases me is that his involvement is a real outgrowth of our youth-ministry program." In this case, the congregation didn't need to be convinced to include a teenager as a deacon just because youth should be represented, but the congregation saw what this teenager was doing and his spiritual maturity, and asked, "Why isn't he a deacon?"

3. What Ages Are Group Members?

Seventh-graders will have different interests and abilities from those of twelfth-graders. Some of the key developmental differences between younger (grades 6–8) and older (grades 9–12) adolescents are described in Figure 6. These characterizations have implications for the design of effective service-learning projects. For younger adolescents, projects must . . .
. . . have very concrete and observable consequences
. . . demand the expenditure of physical activity
. . . provide clear affirmation
. . . involve a group of youth involved in a common task.[10]

Among older adolescents, activity and concreteness are still useful, but less necessary. Effective service projects can be . . .
. . . more directed to the utilization of individual talent
. . . more abstract or indirect in their impact
. . . more targeted to systemic change than relational or face-to-face.

These rather general understandings of adolescent development suggest the following kinds of service projects:

For grades 6-8
• Planting trees in a park
• Setting up a recycling program
• Helping a family move
• Collecting food for a foodshelf
• Helping in a homeless shelter
• Tutoring younger children
• Visiting nursing homes
• Being peer ministers

For grades 9-12
• Designing and conducting a campaign to educate others about the environment
• Writing letters to Congress or city officials
• Organizing a product boycott
• Educating adults about racism
• Teaming with adults to build or renovate a home
• Tutoring younger children
• Running an after-school program

41

Figure 6
Developmental Differences Between
Younger and Older Youth

Areas of Development	Major Developmental Themes	
	Grades 6-8	Grades 9-12
Cognitive	• Concrete thinking • Emphasis is more on the here-and-now, or what one can directly experience	• Abstract thinking emerges. • Can think about ideas and possibilities • More critical of tradition and institutions
Physical Maturation	• Rapid physical changes • A Short attention span • Can be awkward • Girls appear more mature than boys	• Physical changes stabilize • Attention span increases • Boys catch up to girls • Want to be treated more as an adult than a child
Identity	• Looking for sense of group identity • Needs affirmation of parents, other adults, and peers • Emerging self-consciousness	• Looking for sense of personal identity • Tendency to be self-critical • Beginning to evaluate self and think about future
Peer Group	• Strong need to fit in • Sticking out can be painful • Susceptibility to peer pressure increases	• Declining susceptibility to peer pressure • More discriminating about friendship choices
Values and Morality	• High interest in helping • Tendency to view moral issues as black or white • Legalistic	• Strong increase in need for autonomy and independence • Susceptible to hedonism • Emerging understanding of moral principles

Above all else, however, it is important to involve older adolescents in the planning of a service project (per the need for autonomy and independence) and to permit individual interests an outlet. (Younger youth also can be involved in planning, to a lesser degree.) In addition, reflection and debriefing can deal with more complex issues with older youth (see chapter 7).

Another important factor in addressing age differences is what developmental psychologists call "critical periods." These are times in a life cycle that are particularly crucial for learning, because learning is easier during that period, but harder later.

It appears that younger adolescents have a particular readiness to serve. According to data from *The Troubled Journey*, there is a particular readiness and interest during the sixth grade. Thus service-learning is particularly powerful at this age, as it provides a good match with natural inclinations. Service during early adolescence could cement and stabilize a commitment that could, in theory, inhibit the typical slide away from service in late adolescence.

A corollary might be as follows: It is harder to teach service to older adolescents if service was not a program priority during the middle-grade years. This makes service-learning a priority in all years, from grades 6 through 12.

4. How Ready Is Your Group?

Different youth groups are at different levels of readiness for service. Some may have only limited exposure to and interest in service, while others may be seasoned veterans. But the number of mission trips isn't always the best clue to the *real* readiness of the group to serve.

Carol Davis Younger, a youth worker and writer in Kansas, tells about a seasoned suburban youth group that partnered with her inner-city youth group when she worked in Louisville, Kentucky. Her little group, made up primarily of unchurched youth, first felt intimidated by the busload of youth who arrived for the weeklong vacation Bible school. But though the suburban group had been on mission trips every summer for years, it quickly became clear that they were not really ready.

The problems started when the members of the suburban group were assigned to stay in families' homes. They complained because there was no air conditioning, and they didn't feel safe. Many families were embarrassed and angered when some of the young people checked into motels.

And that was just the first of a series of problems. The entire experience was captured in Younger's mind on the last day of the trip, when the suburban group was getting ready to leave. The whole group had lined up to have their picture taken in this urban neighborhood where they had worked. When one of the neighborhood children ran to get into the picture, the teenagers pushed the child away.

Despite all the problems, Younger says that trip had a positive side as well. Her little inner-city group saw itself in a new light. "That experience changed our youth ministry," Younger recalls, "because the kids started seeing themselves as Christians who could serve. It showed them that they could do as much as the kids with a big budget." Her group became active in addressing the needs in their own community. And some of the group members—who might not even have graduated from high school—have continued their education in order to dedicate their lives to serve in the community.

As she has thought about these experiences, Younger uses the analogy of the parable of the soils (Mark 4:1-20) to describe the differences in youth group readiness for service:

- **Hard Path**—These groups don't seem ready to serve at all. They simply haven't heard the call. Younger suggests that you have to start with these groups by softening the ground gradually. This might mean adding a simple service-learning component first, then gradually building on it as the interest grows.
- **Thorny Soil**—These groups are the ones made up of lots of busy youth. You might be able to start service projects, but they get choked out. In these cases, Younger suggests two strategies. One is to find ways to help members serve through some of their existing commitments at school and home—to see some of what they're already doing as ministry, and process it in terms of their faith. Second, she suggests helping young people focus on their commitments and priorities, so they can better learn to weed out the commitments that are choking their spiritual growth.
- **Rocky Soil**—These are those groups that have great initial enthusiasm, but don't sustain it. These groups need particular attention to reflection on the experience so that it becomes integrated into their lives. They may also need more frequent "cultivating" to keep the roots from drying out.
- **Rich Soil**—These youth groups are the ones that are ready for planting. And, as in the parable, Younger says these groups always reap a greater harvest than you would ever have anticipated.

Of course, any single youth group may include members who represent each type of soil. Thus, you are likely to need a different "gardening" technique to reach each one. That's the strategy of the Servant Leadership Project of Zion Baptist Church. At the heart of the project is a core program that draws highly committed youth to a summer of intensive involvement in a variety of issues.

But since only a handful of youth can (or are ready to) make this kind of commitment, the program allows them to sign up for any single week-long project. This approach engages each young person in an area of interest, while also challenging those who are ready for high commitment. In the process, they serve as role models and mentors for other young people.

5. Where Will We Serve?

When you think of service, what is the first thing that comes to mind? Some might first remember a cross-country mission trip. Others might imagine the local homeless shelter. Others might think about making sermon tapes for homebound church members. As these examples show, service can be close to home, or as far from home as you choose. It's important that the advantages and disadvantages of each place be understood as you think through the possibilities.

In the Youth Group—Sometimes we forget the value of the service and compassion shown to one another in the group. The peer-ministry model is a clear example of how effective this service can be. In this program, young people learn to be sensitive to the needs and concerns of those around them, and they develop skills for listening and helping their peers. Other in-group services might include a homework hotline (to get help from a peer) or visits to the homes of sick group members.

Service within the youth program can be extremely valuable, building community and acceptance, and helping young people through difficult times. It can also teach important friendship and leadership skills. Finally, these service efforts can be much easier to plan and coordinate, because they focus only within the program.

The major limitation of service within the youth group is that it can be too close to home. One of the keys to effective service-learning is that young people are stretched beyond their normal surroundings and relationships. Making such bridges occur within the group requires an unusually diverse group. Furthermore, if the youth group focuses all its attention on itself, it risks becoming in-grown and self-absorbed.

In the Congregation—For years, youth groups have served within the congregation—leading in worship, assisting with the children's program, offering assistance to the elderly or people with disabilities, helping with church mailings, cleaning the church grounds, and serving on committees or boards.

Service projects within the congregation can be a good starting point for a service-learning effort. They are easy to arrange, and church members probably will be open and affirming of those who serve them. Furthermore, short service-learning projects often can be done during—or in conjunction with—traditional education times (such as Sunday school or youth group), allowing for immediate debriefing and discussion. Finally, getting young people together with senior citizens can be an important stimulus for faith.

At the same time, service within the congregation has most of the same limitations as service within the youth group. It tends to be with a known set of people, which reduces the sense of risk and stretching, and often, diversity (except age diversity) is difficult to address. Finally, it does not extend the church's ministry into the community or the world.

In the Local Community—You need only read your local newspaper to recognize needs and issues in your community. Whether your congregation is urban, suburban, rural, or small town, the issues of poverty, crisis, illness, aging, injustice, loneliness, illiteracy, racism, violence, and environment (to name just a few) are all alive and in need of attention. Young people can contribute significantly in addressing these concerns.

Research on service-learning suggests that service in the local community should be at the core of a well-rounded effort. Local issues have several key advantages:
- Because the projects can be undertaken locally, they can be supported and sustained over time.
- Young people can be involved for weeks or months, developing relationships and becoming more and more attuned to the issues.
- Debriefing and study can occur over several weeks or months, allowing for more processing and more learning.
- These ministries pull young people out of their world of comfort to address the needs of diverse people. This introduces an important element of risk and challenge.
- Local projects allow for different levels of commitment. Young people may choose to become heavily involved, or they may be involved only occasionally.
- Finally, these projects are easily repeatable and easier to "give away." As young people become involved, they can tell their friends—and bring their friends along. That's more difficult when the service happens only once a year on a long mission trip.

However, there are limitations to service in the local community. On a practical level, it can be difficult initially to motivate and interest young people in serving down the street instead of across the world. And since young people may be involved in many other activities, service may be pushed aside and neglected if it is not made a priority.

Finally, local service usually occurs in one hour here and one hour there. Thus it can lack the heavy impact that an intense, week-long trip away from home can have when young people "live and breathe" the experience. Many youth workers say they have more trouble seeing and naming the impact of local service efforts than of the more intense work camps and mission trips.

In the Nation—Youth workers who involve their groups in service beyond the immediate community, through mission trips and work camps, insist that these efforts have a tremendously positive impact on their groups. As Dean Feldmeyer, a pastor in Ohio says, "Workcamp experiences are among the most impacting experiences in youth ministry."

Venturing beyond your own town or city has a significant impact for several reasons:
- As mentioned earlier, the longer trips allow young people to concentrate on the service experience without many of the distractions they have at home.
- Trips can attract young people who might not otherwise consider service involvement. The chance of getting away from home and going to "exotic" places has a sense of adventure that builds anticipation and enthusiasm.
- They place youth in an unfamiliar environment and culture, which helps them break out of their natural patterns and experiences.
- Being together with other group members for these intense experiences also can bond a youth group in unique and important ways.
- Finally, the longer trip also allows for processing the experience as the work is in progress. Quality work camps and mission trips include times for learning about the local culture, its issues, and how the experience relates to the Christian faith.

These trips beyond the community also have limitations, however:
- They lack the continuity and immediacy of the local projects.
- Because they require a significant block of time, some young people may not be able to participate in the experience because of other commitments.
- They can become rather expensive, making it difficult for some young people to participate.
- Youth groups can become consumed with raising money for a mission or work-camp trip.
- Without careful processing, trips can divide youth groups between those who did and those who did not participate.
- Because of distance, trips can be difficult to plan, unless you connect with an existing program.
- Finally, an overemphasis on trips to other places can give young people the false impression that there are no real needs in their own community.

Young people can become involved in national concerns also through the advocacy of national political issues. By encouraging them to study relevant issues, form articulate opinions, then express those opinions (by demonstrating, writing letters, etc.), youth programs can help young people apply their faith to key national concerns and cultivate a lifelong interest in these issues.[11]

In the World—Ridge Burns tells the story of a youth pastor whose group had just returned from a mission trip to Mexico. The group had been stunned by the generosity of the Mexican people, who were living in extreme poverty, yet wanted to share with these affluent Americans. Burns writes:

> One girl in the group was particularly affected by the contrast in values between the Mexican culture and her own. When the vanloads of kids arrived back at the church in Portland, her father came to pick her up in his Mercedes-Benz. As he pulled up in the luxury sedan, the collision of the different cultures hit her, and she threw up.[12]

This story graphically illustrates the potential impact of an international service project. In addition to the benefits of a work camp in the country, an international focus can broaden young people's perspective even more, as they learn about the cultures, politics, needs, and realities in developing world nations.

At the same time, international service also has the drawbacks of other work camps and mission trips—some of which are exacerbated by greater cost, distance, and perceived risk. Thus, most churches reserve international travel for more experienced and mature youth groups.

Youth groups also may choose to address international issues without leaving town. This can be done through forming local chapters of international organizations (such as Amnesty International), forming a partnership with a youth group in another country, raising money for hunger or other international concerns, supporting a missionary, or sponsoring a child in another country. While these approaches do not have the personal impact of direct contact, they can be concrete connections that build young people's interests and encourage them to learn about world issues.

Of course, your youth group need not choose just one of these approaches or locations for service—particularly once you've established a tradition of involvement. Dave Carver's suburban youth program in Rochester, New York, maintains a three-year cycle. For one year the program concentrates on urban issues, focusing on understanding the people and issues of the inner city, then visiting a city for an urban mission trip. The next year, the program focuses on rural issues, people, and needs, with a work camp experience in Appalachia. In the third year, the focus is international and includes a mission trip to Latin America. And throughout each year, the young people are involved in service in their own community.

6. How Will We Integrate Service-Learning?

As you are reading these possibilities, you may be facing this very real question: How can I fit this into the ministry? You may see the value of having service as part of your Christian-education program, for example, but you feel lucky to get your youth to commit to a 45-minute class each week, much less a full-blown service project. You may also worry about the added challenges of organizing and maintaining a service project in the community, in addition to all your other responsibilities.

The good news is that service-learning can have many roles in a youth ministry, depending on your resources, commitment, group size, goals, and tradition of service. Knowing the options is important in order to avoid the trap of thinking that service-learning can happen only one way. (And hence, if that way doesn't work, then service-learning won't work at all in a particular congregation.)

The good news is that service-learning fits naturally into a congregation's goals and ministry. Congregations don't face many of the barriers that schools face, including existing curriculum requirements that must be met within a limited class period, skepticism among some educators about whether service is appropriate in the school, and debates over mandatory versus voluntary service requirements.

At the same time, your youth program may already be so filled with options and programs that a new program would be inappropriate. You may have a variety of other emphases against which you must balance an emphasis on service. Or you may be struggling to find a focus, and service-learning could be at the heart of a new philosophy of youth ministry for you.

Thus it's useful to explore some of the models for service-learning that have been developed in education, to discover their applicability to the congregation-based youth ministry.[13] Here these are arranged from the least-integrated into the youth ministry's overall curriculum and plan, to the most-integrated.

A "Volunteer Service Clearinghouse"—In this model, the church doesn't actually plan service projects or opportunities, but serves as a clearinghouse for existing opportunities. The youth program might list opportunities in the church newsletter (with phone numbers to call to volunteer), or announce them in youth-group meetings. Individual group members would find opportunities that fit their interests and needs, then involve themselves.

A clearinghouse approach has several advantages. It allows young people to be involved, depending on their own interests and abilities and time commitments. It doesn't require the administration time needed for planning and implementing projects. It works well in groups that aren't large enough to undertake their own projects. Finally, it provides valuable resources to agencies in the city that really need the young people's energy, skills, and enthusiasm.

The approach is limited, however, in its ability to use the experiences for learning and growing (although leaders can intentionally spend one-on-one time talking about the experiences). It also is harder for the youth ministry to support young people in their various ministries, because there is no direct contact. As a result, young people may become discouraged and quit without the youth worker having an opportunity to assess the situation and work to deal with any problems.

Special Programs or Projects—Special-service projects are probably the most common in youth ministry. A group (or person) plans and organizes the project, announces and advertises it, and young people who are interested participate. An annual work camp, mission trip, walk for hunger, spring cleanup, canned-food drive, or other such effort generally fall into this category.

These projects are not integrated into the overall youth-ministry program. In some cases, they are developed by someone (such as the missions committee) with little direct connection to the rest of the youth program, other than scheduling to avoid conflicts.

These kinds of projects can be valuable in a youth-ministry program in many ways. First, they can serve as "entry points" to service, since they often have relatively low commitments. They can also expose young people to a variety of options and issues, without requiring long-term commitment before they have experienced service. Furthermore, by involving young people in the planning of these events, you will find that they learn leadership skills that transfer into other areas. Finally, these projects can be important group-building times for the youth group.

The down side of these opportunities is that they don't provide the continuity and long-term commitment in which true learning and growth are more likely to occur. They also tend to require a lot of planning, compared to the actual time given to service. Finally, since they often aren't integrated into the overall youth ministry, they tend not to be as effective vehicles for learning.

A "Lab" for Christian-education Classes—Some of the same activities may occur here as in some of the earlier models. But here the projects are chosen partly to complement and enhance specific learning objectives. The service component becomes the "reality check" for what is being learned in Sunday school, confirmation, youth group, or other existing educational programs.

This approach doesn't require changes in the existing curriculum, but enhances it. (Some youth curriculum even give suggestions for complementary service projects.) For example, if young people are learning about Christian responsibility for the environment, they might assess the environment in their own neighborhood (on a neighborhood walk), then select particular strategies for addressing significant needs (from launching a recycling program to lobbying for cleanup of a hazardous waste dump).

A Service-based Youth-ministry Program—Some congregations are taking the next step by structuring a complete area of the youth ministry around service-learning. The description from public schools fits the church as well:

> Here the community experience forms the heart and is the central focus for the course, but it is combined with an ongoing classroom experience where the emphasis is on providing information, skills, and generalizing principles to assist students directly in interpreting their experiences to operate more successfully in their [service] placements.[14]

In this model, service would be the organizing principle for youth ministry, or for a specific component, such as confirmation or discipleship training. All Christian education would flow out of reflection on community service. Bible study would grow out of the experiences of group members in service. Through service, young people examine their relationship with God and explore how their faith sustains them. Other programs would be seen in light of this focus as well. In essence, to be part of the youth program would mean being actively involved in service.

Such an approach is close to the one in Ginghamsburg United Methodist Church, where, says youth worker Mike Nygren, service is "a way of life." The church sponsors a wide range of service opportunities—both locally and elsewhere—and most of the rest of the youth program connects to and builds on these efforts. The goal, Nygren says, is to have the youth use their gifts. "They have abilities. . . . We just say to them, 'Let's start doing it.'"

Beginning in seventh grade, the program starts young people on a progression that tells them, "We need you here for six years." To participate in mission trips, young people go through intensive leadership training. Then they, in turn, teach those skills to other teens in the community. The youth-fellowship program—which takes place twenty times a year—spends a lot of time processing events and projects so that young people share and remember the vision of service.

The service emphasis also influences young people's life-style choices. Those who work in the church's after-school Clubhouse program sign an "integrity covenant," which simply says, "My life-style is something I would like little children to know about." That statement becomes the focus for conversation and study about values, beliefs, and behaviors.

Churchwide Focus—Your congregation could choose to make an issue, project, or theme an emphasis across all ages. In this way, children, youth, and adults all engage in similar action, creating an energy and focus in the congregation. This approach also gives the opportunity to see significant impact on a particular issue or need because of the church's effort.

7. Partnerships, or Solo?

Another key decision to be made in a service-learning program is whether to design and implement your own ministries or partner with existing programs. Often youth ministries can build on the experience of community organizations (food pantries, United Way, mentoring programs), and turn to these organizations to learn about the issues surrounding particular needs. Linking with national work camp or missions organizations also can reduce the likelihood of problems at a work camp, and these organizations often have materials prepared for preparation and debriefing. Or several youth programs could join together in a ministry effort, with leadership, responsibility, and support being shared by everyone.

Another logical option is to partner with public schools in the community, particularly if the schools have community service as part of their programming. By jointly sponsoring or coordinating projects that address the hoped-for outcome for both the school and the congregation, the youth are allowed to focus their energy. Then they can reflectively process the experience, both from the knowledge base of the schools and from the theological base of the church. Neither institution needs to convince the other; rather, the young people learn to think about one experience in different ways (theologically and scientifically).

Many factors can influence this decision, and the following questions may help clarify your choices:

- Are others already doing an effective job in organizing and administering the kind of service we would like to perform? Would another program simply duplicate efforts?
- Do we have the resources, skills, and energy to develop—and sustain—our own programs?
- What level of organization and management does a particular project need?
- Would a program run by our youth ministry offer distinct advantages to the community (such as a spiritual emphasis, more person-to-person contact, etc.)?
- Are our young people adequately prepared to develop and lead their own efforts?
- Do the benefits of managing our own program (sense of ownership, meeting unmet needs, teaching leadership skills, building visibility in the community) outweigh the costs and the risks?

Each congregation will answer these questions differently. In most cases, small groups and groups with less service experience would be well-advised to link with other agencies and existing services. More experienced groups may find that their young people have developed the skills, commitments, and resources to develop a unique program.

Another option should not be overlooked: Young people could become volunteers in service ministries of the whole congregation. They would not only have opportunities to participate in service, but could also serve on the planning and coordinating groups for these congregation-wide ministries.

Every Saturday afternoon, people from Kirkwood Baptist Church in St. Louis, Missouri, help run a soup kitchen at an inner-city church. Young people work side-by-side with the adults in this ministry. Not only are the young exposed to poverty in their own city, says Associate Pastor and Minister of Youth Jeff Allee, but "people they didn't know in the congregation, they now have rolled up their sleeves and worked with."

8. Service, or Justice?

Most youth ministries—indeed, most congregations—focus their outreach efforts on meeting direct human needs: caring for the poor, sick, vulnerable. Yet most people who become involved in service see an unbreakable link between service and justice: advocating for change in the systems that perpetuate inequities and misplaced priorities in our world.

In *Acts of Compassion*, Robert Wuthnow explored the relationship between service (or compassion) and justice, based on extensive research and surveys of compassionate people:

> Some have argued that compassion and a concern for social justice are quite different. The compassionate person, in this view, must be willing to give up his or her rights. Compassion requires a focus on relationships, on what two individuals together can accomplish. Justice, in

contrast, is intensely focused on the rights of individuals. It focuses less on the happy merging and blending of two individuals, and more on each jealously standing up for the dignity and autonomy of the other.[15]

Developmentally, thinking about and understanding justice requires the ability to think abstractly, an ability that emerges in later adolescence.

It may be, however, that too much is made of this distinction—that service and justice complement and build on each other. It seems appropriate—both theologically and practically—to strive for a link between service and justice in youth's service-learning efforts. As the youth meet the personal needs of individuals, they need to learn about the systems that contribute to perpetuating the needs and take away those individuals' rights. And as they learn about these systems, they need opportunities to advocate for changes that address the injustices. Anthony Campolo puts the challenge this way in *Ideas for Social Action:*

> It is vitally important that Christians be involved in ministry to those who are suffering and who are oppressed. This is our highest priority. But there is also truth in the belief that it does little good to minister to the victims of an evil system while doing nothing at all to change that system so that it produces fewer victims.[16]

Whether the focus is on service or on justice, however, the key to remember is that young people need to become directly involved, not abstractly interested. It is when issues become concrete and personal that they become real. "Direct service work can be seen as just the first in a series of developmental steps of the service-learning program," writes Jane Kendall. For example, some youth may serve in a soup kitchen. Upon reflection, they begin to ask why people are hungry, which provides an opening to learn about larger social and political forces, perhaps through service-learning in an advocacy group or a government agency. Later, the youth group might take an international work camp, which would broaden the issue to a global one.

Kendall concludes: "These later steps in the service-learning continuum are important for skill-building and awareness related to social concerns that youth need to carry into adult life as responsible members of local and global communities."[17] And, we would add, as responsible Christians.

While direct service is a vital component, justice and advocacy can enrich a youth ministry by teaching young people important lessons about their responsibility as Christians in their community. The experience of Shiloh Baptist Church in Trenton, New Jersey, illustrates this. Because of the congregation's inner-city environment, says youthworker Buster Soaries, "Our kids are in trouble simply by virtue of where they are born. We've got to deal with the systemic evils that oppress our kids."

Thus the congregation actively follows local, state, and national issues that affect young people. And when an issue is close to home, the youth group takes action. Once the city council was voting on whether to close the only library in the church's low-income neighborhood. The young people prepared statements about why the library shouldn't be closed and how it would affect them. Then they went en masse to city hall for the hearing. Their impact was profound, and the library stayed open.[18]

9. Short-term, or Ongoing?

One of the underlying problems concerning service in youth ministry is the tension between the one-time projects and the ongoing efforts. The literature on service-learning shows a clear preference for ongoing projects, in which young people are exposed to an issue and process the experience over several months. This approach allows relationships to form, values to shift, and lifelong skills to develop.

Dean Feldmeyer, a United Methodist pastor, tells about a youth group in a former congregation where the young people visited the nursing home monthly to lead recreation and make friends. As the weeks passed, young people began building strong relationships with "someone completely out of their frame of experience." They would send cards and call on the phone between visits. If one of the "regulars" was missing from a recreation time, the youth would go searching through the nursing home to find the person.

These close relationships also lead to significant learning. Not only did the youth hear the stories and perspectives of another generation, they also struggled with issues of death and dying when their friends in the home passed away.

At the same time, youth ministers find that many one-time experiences can have a significant impact in their youth program. Particularly valuable are immersion experiences such as a work camp, urban plunge, or mission trip. As Thomas J. Bright observes, "Working and/or living among poor and marginalized persons is to experience the impact of injustice on people's lives firsthand and to turn our energy into creative healthy alternatives for them."[19]

The most effective programs find a balance of the two approaches. One-time projects in the community are used as entry points for youth who haven't been involved. Work camps and mission trips are designed to inspire, motivate, and sustain young people. And finally, ongoing ministries allow for building relationships and learning about issues in depth. In any case, individual short-term projects clearly will not have a lasting impact on their own, as Lyn Baird states:

> Service-learning achieves its full value only if it leads to an enduring life-style of continued personal development and concern for others. A one-shot inoculation will not provide lasting immunization against the social malady of self-interest. The impulse to serve needs to be nurtured over time.[20]

10. How Can We Include Families?

We have repeatedly made the point that service-learning in the congregation can have a profound influence on nurturing values and faith. But we should also remember that parents remain the ultimate influence on values and faith. Service-learning programs become doubly powerful, then, if congregations build families into the enterprise.[21] This can involve several strategies:
  • Teach families how to design and implement their own service projects;
  • Draw several families together to share service;
  • Incorporate parents into the youth-ministry service-learning program.

Our Father Lutheran Church in Denver, Colorado, seeks to make family service a regular part of its ministry. Once a month, families meet after worship on Sunday. They go out to lunch at a restaurant in the community, where they'll work, then spend the afternoon in some kind of ministry. Usually they begin by touring the ministry to learn about its work and philosophy. Then they undertake projects together. Families invite other families, and the circle of involvement grows.

Throughout this chapter, we have presented options in service-learning as either/or questions: either service or justice; either short-term or long-term. In reality, however, these options can be integrated in ways that complement each other. All it requires is coordination and planning. Figure 7 shows some ways the different levels of involvement can work together. The next chapter suggests a step-by-step process for developing a service-learning program in your own youth ministry.

Figure 7
Integrating Service Options into Youth Ministry

Educational objective	Short-term local projects	Ongoing local projects	Mission trips and workcamps	Advocacy and social justice
To explore the biblical mandate to care for the poor and hungry	• Participate in (or organize) a canned food drive • Help repair or build a home through Habitat for Humanity	• Plant gardens for low-income and elderly people • Participate in a mentoring program that reaches low-income children	• Spend a week gleaning food for a food pantry • Go on a workcamp to repair homes in an urban or rural community	• Work with Bread for the World • Prepare newsletters or skits to raise awareness of hunger issues
To understand the Christian's responsibility for creation	• Plant trees in a city park on Arbor Day • Develop sheets to tell church members how to protect the environment	• Become responsible for maintaining a stretch of highway • Coordinate a recycling program in the church	• Help an urban neighborhood plant a garden in a vacant lot • Assist with re-forestation efforts in a developing nation	• Test water in a local lake or river and advocate for cleanup • Hold a fundraiser to buy part of a rainforest
To learn Christian care-giving skills	• Deliver "care packages" to nursing home or prison • Collect the oral histories of members who model Christian care-giving	• Start a peer ministry program • Form a prayer chain to pray for people in the youth group • Regularly visit a nursing home	• Lead a vacation church school in an urban neighborhood • Do repairs, cleanup, or recreation at a home for difficult children	• Advocate for humane living conditions in prisons • Volunteer in an AIDS ward in a hospital or hospice
To learn about Christian leadership	• Create and conduct a survey of the congregation to assess leadership skills and needs	• Teach children in Sunday school or other programs • Become interns with church members to assist them in their professions	• Volunteer as leaders in a camp for children with disabling conditions • Lead vacation Bible school for inner-city children	• Hold a diversity fair for the congregation • Talk to city council about how one's city responds to homelessness
To develop responsible values regarding alcohol and other drugs	• Sponsor an alcohol/drug-free prom party for a high school • Join with other local youth organizations to have a Chemical Awareness Week	• Train for and staff a hotline for youth having problems with alcohol/drugs • Form a band or rap group that advocates healthy lifestyles in its music	• Do a cleanup project for a mission facility that seeks to deal with addictions • Write and produce a drama that you take on tour across your state	• Investigate local merchants that sell alcohol and cigarettes to minors • Lobby city council to make alcohol less accessible to minors
To learn about Christ's call to be peacemakers	• Participate in a walk to raise awareness about violence in the community • Train and lead a workshop on how to prevent sexual harrassment	• Learn mediation and nonviolence skills to defuse violent situations in school • Become pen pals with young people in other parts of the world	• Go on a relief mission to a country recently in conflict • Organize and lead activities for children in violent urban neighborhoods	• Campaign for stiffer laws against sexual harassment • Make video of concerns about violence in the community. Show it to the city council

4 BUILDING YOUR PROGRAM: CHOOSING A PROJECT

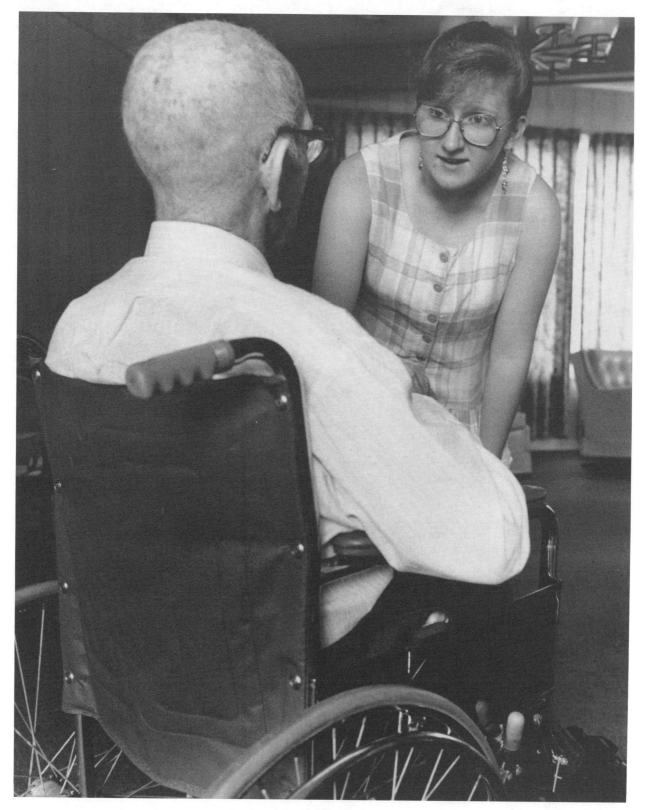

For this month's service project at Neighborhood Family Church, the youth will gather cans of food for the local food pantry. The creative youth minister divides the group into teams and turns them loose to see which one can collect the most cans. The winning team would be given a pizza party by all the other teams. The group collects 1,000 pounds of food—and has a lot of fun doing it. The youth minister delivers the food to the pantry, then has the thank-you letter from the pantry printed in the church newsletter.

Across town, the youth group at Main Street Church is also holding a canned-food drive for the food pantry. But this isn't just the latest in a string of unrelated service projects. Three months earlier, the confirmation class had spent a Saturday afternoon walking through a low-income neighborhood near the church. As they walked, the youth leader had asked questions: "What kinds of stores do you see here? What businesses do you see here where people can work? What are the streets like? How do the food prices compare to the grocery store where your family shops?" Before the end of the afternoon, the teenagers had talked with an unemployed father, a single mother, two teenagers who had dropped out of school, and the director of a church-related community center in the neighborhood.

Their next three Sunday school classes had focused on Christian concern for the poor. The young people were assigned to do reading and interviewing during the week. In their journals, they noted what they were learning and how that had affected their values and faith. At the next confirmation class, the group began to ask, What can we do? They explored possibilities, remembered conversations from the neighborhood walk, and talked about goals.

Since they wanted to begin by raising awareness in the whole congregation, they launched the canned-food drive. During announcements at the end of worship services, they told about their experiences on the neighborhood walk and about their research. They printed excerpts from their journals in the church newsletter. They visited the children's Sunday school classes to tell them how they could help others.

In the end, this group also collected 1,000 pounds of food for the pantry. The next Saturday, the group spent the morning putting the cans on the shelves and talking with the pantry staff and volunteers. What kind of people come for food? Why are people hungry in our own city when we have so much? Why do poor people eat so much junk food? And the answers and stories introduced the inquirers to the complex issues that surround hunger and poverty in the United States—and the ways Christians are called to address the issues.

You might say that both groups accomplished the same goal: They collected 1,000 pounds of food. But which approach was more likely to change the lives and thinking of the young people? Which group was more likely to do another project? . . . and another? . . . and another?

The Pitfalls of Service

Simply getting the youth involved in service is no guarantee of a positive experience. In fact, poorly planned or executed service experiences can backfire. And some youth workers fear that although being involved in service is now in vogue, it won't substantially change people's perspectives, life-styles, or priorities. "I'm not sure what the motivations are," says Jeff Allee, associate pastor and minister with youth at Kirkwood Baptist Church in Kirkwood, Missouri. "I'm not sure we think of poor people any differently. I'm concerned that we're not changing our worldviews . . . to understand how our life-style contributes to the problems."

In looking back to other times when service was in vogue, Jane C. Kendall notes three primary lessons that are essential to learn from and build upon—and which readily apply to youth ministry:

- Most of the programs were not integrated into the organizations where they were based.
- Good intentions do no always translate into good (that is, appropriate) deeds.
- While service can be a powerful vehicle for education, "Learning from service experiences is not automatic or easy to facilitate."[1]

10 Keys to Effective Service-Learning

Recognizing the danger of poorly done service experiences, a broad-based group of experiential educators from 75 national and regional organizations began to pull together their shared wisdom about what works and what doesn't work in service-learning. Then they came together in a collaborative process to identify ten "Principles of Good Practice in Combining Service and Learning." These principles are an important foundation for designing service-learning programs in your youth ministry:

1. *Engage in responsible and sustained actions for the common good.* Effective service-learning projects engage in important, ongoing work, so that positive, lasting change is possible. Though one-time projects or work camps have an important place in an overall youth-ministry service program, these efforts are less effective, both as vehicles for learning and as contributors to society. Furthermore, it's important that these projects involve real, important work, not contrived work that young people can see is not meaningful for anyone.

2. *Provide structured opportunities for young people to reflect critically on their service experience.* "The service experienced alone does not ensure that either significant learning or effective service will occur," the guidelines explain. "It is important that programs build in structured opportunities for participants to think about their experience and what they are doing." Chapter 7 focuses on debriefing and application.

3. *Articulate clear service and learning goals.* Both participants and recipients need to have a clear, mutual understanding of what is to be accomplished and what is to be learned through the experience. Such mutuality helps keep the service from becoming patronizing.

4. *Allow for those in need to define those needs.* This principle guards against resentment among recipients when projects take away jobs from the local community or their results are not seen as useful. Involving community leaders, agencies, and individuals in the planning process ensures that the project is indeed appropriate and valuable for the local community. Youth groups must develop a mindset of reciprocity, in which they work together with those being served, with each learning from the other. In *Servant Leadership*, Robert Greenleaf makes a challenge that applies here:

> The difference manifests itself in the care taken by the [servant leader] to make sure that other people's highest priority needs are being served. The best test, and most difficult to administer, is: Do those served grow as persons? Do they, *while being served*, become healthier, wiser, freer, more autonomous, more likely themselves to become servants? *And*, what is the effect on the least privileged in society; will they benefit, or at least, not be further deprived?[2]

5. *Clarify responsibilities.* Each person and each organization should have clearly defined roles. These could include youth-group members, adult sponsors, community leaders, sponsoring organizations, and the people and organizations receiving service. This negotiation should involve not only responsibility for tasks, but also acknowledgment of the values and principles of everyone involved.

6. *Recognize changing circumstances as you match service providers and service needs.* Effective service-learning begins by carefully matching service providers with appropriate service needs. Furthermore, since the service experience often changes people's values and priorities, projects need continual feedback and evaluation, as relationships, needs, and perspectives change. Such flexibility can lead to surprising innovative outcomes.

7. *Expect genuine, active, and sustained organizational commitment.* Projects inevitably fizzle out when organizations no longer consider them important. Thus, sponsoring and receiving organizations must make a strong, lasting commitment to the service-learning goals in order for the process to be effective.

8. *Include training, supervision, monitoring, support, recognition, and evaluation to meet service and learning goals.* Each of these activities supports and nourishes those who serve by giving them the skills they need to grow in their work, and by recognizing that they are, indeed, making an important contribution.

9. *Ensure that the time commitment is flexible, appropriate, and in the best interest of all involved.* If projects demand more time than is practical in the busy world of adolescents, the effort is likely to be abandoned. If too little is demanded, the service may become trivial and meaningless. Negotiating an appropriate balance and schedule is important to effective service-learning planning.

10. *Commit to program participation by and with diverse populations.* All young people can serve, and all young people can benefit from serving others. Efforts should be made to break down barriers that prevent people from serving. These barriers might include race/ethnicity, religious background, or economic situation, as well as more subtle barriers such as lack of transportation.[3]

These ten principles are a valuable framework for evaluating potential service-learning strategies and projects in your youth program. Once you have this basic framework in mind, you can begin to think specifically about how to build an effective program.

The remainder of this chapter surveys some basic steps you can follow in designing your effort. While these are organized as a step-by-step process, you may find that a different order works for you. Furthermore, this process will likely take several months to complete, and you may find yourself spending even more time on specific areas, depending upon your particular situation. And you may find yourself coming back to different stages at different times, as you begin specific projects. While a description in a book is necessarily linear, reality probably is more cyclical.

Share Your Vision

Just as you have discovered the potential for service-learning in your congregation and youth ministry, you need others to catch the same vision. Otherwise, you'll have difficulty getting support, interest, and involvement. And you'll miss the opportunity to involve the youth in planning and development. The vision should capture people's imagination about how your program could be better by integrating service-learning. These questions may help you articulate your vision:

- How would Christian education be different in your church if young people used their skills and learning to apply their faith in the community?
- How will others feel about your church if young people are acting out their faith in your community by helping the elderly or teaching the young?

57

 • How would members of your youth group feel if they were making a difference in the community by building homes for the homeless or cleaning up the environment?[4]

How can you help church leaders and members, the youth, and others catch a vision of service-learning? You could lead them through a visioning process in which they create pictures about the kind of future they would like to see for young people.[5] You might also take field trips to view other programs, where you could talk with people about the possibilities and see successful models.

Another approach is to introduce elements of service-learning slowly into existing youth programs. For example, if you already sponsor a work camp, add a more intentional reflection component—one that includes journaling, Bible study, and personal sharing (see chapter 7). Then have the young people report to others on the impact of the experience. Quote (with permission) from their journals in the church newsletter. In short, help young people experience the potential, then build on your successes.

Identify and Involve Leadership

While it can be much easier to do all the work of planning yourself, it's imperative to build a base of leadership and ownership among young people, parents, church members, and other leaders. (See chapter 6 on leadership roles for youth.) In fact, it can be counterproductive to "do for" teenagers a program that is supposed to empower them to be responsible contributors and leaders. Furthermore, if a program depends entirely upon the energy and enthusiasm of one leader, it inevitably will flounder if that leader should burn out or leave the church (too-common realities in youth ministry).

Some in youth ministry believe that adults must take primary leadership for programs. But leaders in service-learning strongly argue otherwise, and their experience suggests that congregations often underestimate what their youth can do. Mike Nygren of Ginghamsburg Church writes:

> I am spellbound by the excellence of teens. . . . I have watched them build jungle gyms, run Vacation Bible Schools, build walls, paint murals, plan dinners, conduct parties for children, and the list goes on and on. . . . Their energies, their talents, and their love are just waiting to find a place to be used. In the church we can miss these opportunities because we offer them such boring experiences, or possibly we offer them nothing at all.[6]

In building a leadership team for service-learning, think of the different people and the different roles they will play. What does the youth- or Christian-education director do? What about the young people themselves? What about parents and adult volunteers? What about the pastor? Divide responsibilities according to interests and skills in order to assure that the project is successful and empowering. Bring everyone together early in the process to build shared ownership and to benefit from their insights and commitment.

Bring your leaders together to talk about the vision and make some initial decisions, such as the ten major questions outlined in chapter 3. (Some of these decisions will need to wait until some or all of the assessment is done, but you can at least begin asking the questions together.)

Assess the Situation

At this point, you've brought together a vision for service-learning with the key youth and adult leaders who are interested and committed to the idea. Now it's time to get specific about what you hope to accomplish. To do this, your group must assess (formally or informally) your current situation. Your basic question is this: If young people were available to address needs and solve problems in this community, what would they be doing?

Assessing your situation can be as complicated or as simple as your planning group chooses. If you're starting on a relatively small scale to build a track record, you may need only some conversations with a few people in the youth group, congregation, and community to gather enough information to get started. The questions in Figure 8 can provide a framework for these discussions.

If you're planning a more formal, comprehensive program, in which you're asking your congregation to invest significant time and resources, you'll probably need to conduct more formal assessments.[7] These might include . . .

. . . surveying your youth group and congregation;
. . . researching trends and needs in the community;
. . . auditing existing community resources and organizations;
. . . interviewing community leaders, agency personnel, and experts;
. . . studying the local newspaper;
. . . interviewing community residents.

This assessment can be quite effective if it is led by the youth as a service project in itself. Once your leadership team of young people and adults has determined what information it needs to develop an effective service-learning program, the young people can be trained and released to do the research. In the process, they will learn . . .

. . . some basic research techniques, such as interviewing (over the phone and in person), taking a survey, interviewing, walking through and observing a neighborhood, or researching the key national or global issues that have been selected;
. . . social skills as they interact with others;
. . . planning skills in assessing a situation;
. . . how their faith can be put into action to address needs in the world.

Evaluate the Options

In your community assessment, your planning group uncovered more needs that you could effectively meet. In your youth group assessment, you discovered strengths, interests, and limitations. And you found similar things in your congregation. Now it's time to juxtapose these realities against the group's vision for service-learning, in order to develop objectives. Specifically, what does the group hope to accomplish, and how will you do it?

As you brainstorm and evaluate the possibilities, it's easy to become overwhelmed or get caught up in an idea that may be not be an appropriate match to your group or to the community's needs. One way to reduce this danger is to develop a systematic process for assimilating and evaluating the information. Here is one option for doing this:

1. *Distill the concerns and strengths.* As a leadership group, review the information you've gathered and begin two lists—one for things that concern you and one for things that are encouraging. Then, through consensus, narrow the lists down to three or four top issues and strengths (both in the community and in the church).

2. *Post the lists of top concerns and strengths.* When everyone can see the lists, brainstorm the ways your youth group's resources and strengths could address the top concerns you identified in your community. Write down every idea, and let your imagination flow freely. Once you have a good list with a lot of variety, work toward a consensus of the eight to ten ideas that seem most promising.

3. *Reflect on your congregation's values and history.* How do these affect your selection process?

4. *Define criteria for project selection.* Go back to your vision for service-learning to identify your priorities. Review the ten principles for effective service-learning that opened this chapter. On newsprint, list the things that are most important to you.

5. *Evaluate your program priorities in light of your criteria.* You may want to create a matrix, with the criteria listed in the left margin and the potential projects across the top. Then evaluate each project, using a scoring system (such as a 5-point scale). Or make a copy of Figure 9 to evaluate each project.

6. *Select the two or three projects that appear to have the most potential.*

Figure 8
Assessing Your Needs for Service-Learning

Before planning a service-learning effort, it's important to assess several factors that will influence your choices. Use these questions to help your planning group divide responsibilities and gather the basic information.

Assessing Your Youth Group

1. What are the resources and experiences in the group that can be built on?
2. What is the youth program's sense of calling and vocation to service?
3. What needs in the group do we most want to address?
4. What area of learning do we most want to affect through service-learning?
5. What interests in the group will lend themselves to service projects?
6. What existing leadership in the group can we tap for this effort?
7. What is the developmental level of the group?
8. What obstacles in the group will we confront in implementing service-learning?

Assessing Your Congregation

1. What is the congregation's perception of the current youth program?
2. What is the congregation's current commitment to service?
3. What service experiences in the congregation can we build on?
4. How much support will the congregation give this effort?
5. What resources are in the congregation?
6. How would this effort best support the congregation's overall mission?
7. Are there existing ministries in the congregation to which this effort should connect?

Assessing Your Community

(You may define "community" as your neighborhood, city, nation, or the world, depending upon your focus.)

1. What are the most pressing needs in the community (from the perspective of the youth in your program, as well as from the community's perspective)?
2. What does your church have to say and offer to these pressing issues?
3. What institutions and individuals seeking to meet needs are already in your community? Will these organizations be partners, allies, or adversaries?

Figure 9
Evaluating Potential Service-Learning Projects

How well do your service-project options meet the basic guidelines suggested in the "Principles of Good Practice in Combining Service and Learning" developed by a coalition of experiential educators? While some of those criteria can be met with almost any project, provided it is well-planned, it's still important to ask the questions. Add other criteria that are particularly important to you and your congregation. Make enough copies of this sheet so that you can rate each proposed project. Then use the sheets to evaluate how well the options meet the criteria, on a scale of 1 (not well at all) to 5 (very well).

Name of Project: _____

1. How well does the project engage young people in responsible and sustained actions for the common good? ... 1 2 3 4 5

2. How well does the project provide structured opportunities for teenagers to reflect critically on their service experience? ... 1 2 3 4 5

3. How well does the project articulate clear service and learning goals? ... 1 2 3 4 5

4. How well does the project allow for those in need to define those needs? ... 1 2 3 4 5

5. How clear are the responsibilities defined for the different people and groups involved? ... 1 2 3 4 5

6. How well does the project recognize and allow for changing circumstances, as you match service providers and service needs? ... 1 2 3 4 5

7. How much genuine, active, and sustained organizational commitment does the project have (from the youth group, the church, other participating groups)? ... 1 2 3 4 5

8. How well does the project include training, supervision, monitoring, support, recognition, and evaluation, to meet service and learning goals? ... 1 2 3 4 5

9. How well does the project ensure that the time commitment is flexible, appropriate, and in the best interest of all involved? ... 1 2 3 4 5

10. How well is the project committed to program participation by and with diverse populations? ... 1 2 3 4 5

11. Other: ... 1 2 3 4 5

12. Other: ... 1 2 3 4 5

13. Other: ... 1 2 3 4 5

TOTAL SCORE: _____

Double-check Feasibility of Possible Projects

Even though you have narrowed down the possibilities and have done a thorough assessment, you may not be ready for a final project choice. Let the ideas incubate. Test them on people in the youth group, congregation, and community, to find their reaction. Do some ring true with the congregation's values while others do not? See which ones elicit excitement, and which ones evoke cautions.

Meanwhile, do a bit more research. Talk with potential partners in the community to assess their interest. Investigate the kinds of resources needed, and whether they will be available. Try to gauge commitment to the ideas. In this process, you may modify your original plans to make them stronger. And you will very likely determine that one of the ideas (or maybe a constellation of ideas, if you're more experienced in service) really captures people's imagination and builds on your resources in exciting ways.

5 BUILDING YOUR PROGRAM: THE NUTS AND BOLTS

Now you have a project in mind. People are excited about the potential. It's time to make it happen. Where do you start? What must you do to make the effort successful? Because of the diversity of possible projects and structures—from encouraging one-to-one tutoring with elementary students to an overseas mission trip—it's impossible to outline a step-by-step planning process that will work for your situation.

That does not mean, of course, that you must start from scratch. Several people on the leadership team probably have the skills to shape these step-by-step plans. Or if you're working with an existing program or agency such as Habitat for Humanity or United Way, or a local tutoring program, these organizations usually have suggested schedules and processes that you can use. Furthermore, there are several books on the market that give detailed, step-by-step planning suggestions for projects.[1]

Briefly, then, here are some of the key issues you'll need to address. We've presented them in a simplified, linear way, but you may find that reality is much more interwoven and complicated.

Build and Deploy the Planning Team

Your planning team for a specific project may or may not be the same as your original team. You'll probably want to add someone from the agency you're working with, as well as residents of the community you'll be serving. Some of your original team members may not have the specific skills you need for this project, and they may choose to work elsewhere. Before moving too far into the process, discuss these options and lay out specific roles and responsibilities. Chapter 5 focuses on these leadership issues.

Define Service Objectives

How will your service benefit the community? What needs will it meet? What will the impact be? As a team, agree to your basic objectives so that you can plan with them in mind—and so that later, you can evaluate how well your effort met the objectives.

For example, the youth of Trinity Lutheran Church in Union City, Indiana, established Teen Line Support Services to develop and provide caring, confidential, supportive services, through a hotline at least twelve hours a week, to address the unmet needs of youth. In this case, the service (hotline), the time commitment (12 hours a week), and the audience (teens who need a listening ear) are all clearly stated.

Be sure to include those receiving the service in this decision. Otherwise, you risk meeting needs that don't exist or patronizing and using people to meet your group's own needs. A retirement community director complained, "I am so tired of youth groups coming to sing Christmas carols throughout December, along with bringing the traditional gifts to the elderly." The residents don't need gifts in December, he said—they need friendships all year long.

After hearing that perspective, a youth group rethought its ministry with senior citizens. Now small teams from the youth group go to a nursing home for a very simple task: to talk one of the "regulars" into a game of pool, to join a card game, or, most important, to listen and learn from the people. Young people go primed to ask questions—or maybe to answer a lot of questions. "We go with the goal of sharing a conversation, maybe a laugh, or maybe a memory," writes Mike Nygren. "We try to teach the teens to do what Jesus would do if He visited the center on a rainy Tuesday morning."[2]

The point is not that a particular type of service is, by definition, inappropriate. The point is to really listen to those being served and let their needs and perspectives shape the service choices. Then it's time to move forward with planning the specific project and building it into a quality service and learning experience.

Define Learning Objectives

While the service objectives focus on the service recipient, learning objectives focus on the youth who serve. In the case of the Teen Line Support Services, the objectives for the youth might include learning how to listen, how to support friends in crisis, and the Christian call to befriend those in need. These objectives can help to guide your planned reflection, study, and debriefing around the service project (discussed in chapter 7).

You may also choose to start with the learning objectives of an existing Christian education program, such as the youth fellowship group or confirmation. Identify which of those goals might be best accomplished or enhanced by adding a service-learning component. This approach moves you toward the goal of a Christian education program with service-learning at its core, as an integral and integrated strategy.

Form Partnerships for Service

Much of your planning will be reduced if your group chooses to link with an existing community agency or organization. By building a network in the community where you have contacts with hospitals, schools, and other organizations, you can open doors to potential partners. Partnerships can take many forms:
- Suggest that the youth (as a group or individually) volunteer as part of an agency's existing program;
- Join with an agency or other congregations to start and operate a joint project;
- Use an organization's model, resources, structure, and training to undertake a project such as a Habitat for Humanity house;
- Attend a work camp or mission trip sponsored by an organization or denomination.

Whatever the form of your partnership or relationship, a series of important issues should be addressed, to ensure that the relationship is rewarding for the young people, the agency, the community, and the congregation. Here are some basic suggestions:
- Make sure the organization knows about your church, your youth, your program, and your values, and feels comfortable working with you;
- Make sure you know enough about the agency, its mission and services, its values, and its clients to feel comfortable working with it;
- Offer to provide resources that would become added expenses to the agency if your youth were to volunteer (such as photocopying training materials);
- Be ready to visit at least three times before finalizing commitments. It can take that long to get beyond superficial, guarded conversations.
- Insist that the agency not simply give busy work to the youth. Share your goals and expectations for challenge and learning.

- Clarify expectations for the agency, the young people, and the church, regarding issues such as time commitments, orientation, training, supervision, discipline, roles, placement, transportation, insurance, publicity (if any), and liability.[3]

Many youth workers find that it is quite valuable to build an ongoing relationship with agencies. "Building relationships builds the quality of the kinds of experiences," says Philip Hannam of Zion Baptist Church in Minneapolis. The agencies come to understand your needs, and you learn the agencies' expectations. Furthermore, your youth group will build on the previous years' experiences. Even if the same people don't participate each year, the groups still can get together to talk about the same people and places.

Even if you travel for service, an ongoing relationship can be valuable for sustaining commitment and interest. The youth at Seventh and James Baptist Church in Waco, Texas, send contributions each year to the places where they previously worked, says youth worker Beverly CroweTipton.

Whether you're sending a group to an established work camp program, placing the youth through a local agency to be tutors, or offering services in a nursing home, it's important to ask basic questions about the match between your service-learning needs and the potential agency.

Service-learning educators in a workshop sponsored by the National Center for Service-Learning developed the set of questions shown in Figure 10.[4] These questions can help you sort through the multiple requests and needs, to determine the most effective partnership for you, the kind of agency with which it would be appropriate to work closely.

As a planning group, you may also want to discuss these suggested criteria to see how they fit your own values—and which are most important to you. Your group might, for example, want to ask about the organization's religious ties and perspective. Mark your answer to each question on a scale from 5 (yes, definitely) to 1 (not at all).

Define Tasks and Set Timelines

The tasks and timelines tell you how and when you will get from here to there, and who is going to do what. Your specific tasks will vary with each project, but may include issues of recruitment, training, publicity, fund-raising, scheduling, transportation, and supplies. If your group will participate in an existing program, some of these details will be minimal. But if you are planning an overseas trip, they'll be significant.

Throughout the preparation, the coordinator should check in occasionally with everyone, to be sure that all the pieces are being completed. Nothing will undercut a home-repair work camp more than arriving at the site only to learn that the local materials supplier didn't deliver any boards, paint, or nails.

Keep the Congregation Informed and Involved

Remember how important congregational support will be to this effort—and to others that follow. Find ways to create a sense of ownership and enthusiasm. You might, for example, tap various church members with particular expertise to help plan or to consult on a particular area of the project (a lawyer on liability; a carpenter on building techniques), or to provide training (a teacher on how to lead activities with young children; a furloughing missionary on cross-cultural ministry). Look back at chapter 3 for more ideas about building support in the congregation.

Figure 10
Criteria for Selecting an Agency Partner

Name of Agency/Organization: _____

1. Are those for whom the service is intended part of the
   decision-making process?   5   4   3   2   1

2. Is the organization addressing an issue your service-
   learning program is working on?   5   4   3   2   1

3. Are the organization's mission, goals, and objectives
   clearly stated, and is the organization periodically
   evaluated on the basis of these goals and objectives?   5   4   3   2   1

4. How is the organization funded?   5   4   3   2   1

5. Is the organization working on both the causes and
   the symptoms of the community problems?   5   4   3   2   1

6. Who in the congregation will be orienting, supervising,
   and monitoring the youth? Is this a good match?   5   4   3   2   1

7. Other: 5   4   3   2   1

Explore Liability Issues

Part of the value of service-learning is that it takes young people out of comfortable patterns and challenges them with new settings and risks. However, there is also the potential of injury in work projects, which raises issues of liability. Indeed, according to *Education Week,* many school districts have curtailed outings because of the risks, and one out of ten schools no longer goes on field trips because of the skyrocketing liability insurance premiums.[5]

Congregations involved in service projects, mission trips, and work camps should obtain solid legal advice from lawyers in determining how to deal with these issues. Here are some of the common issues that must be addressed.[6] (The recommendations here do not constitute legal advice, but represent the way many congregations deal with some of the issues.)

Transportation—Whether your project is local or across the country, transportation responsibility, safety, and insurance issues must be resolved. Who will drive what vehicles? What is your policy on seat belts and rowdiness? Whenever possible, use bonded drivers. If you choose to use parents or older students, have clear understandings about liability, insurance, driver's licenses, and seat-belt use. Explore whether the congregation should purchase supplemental insurance. And offer orientation to drivers to be sure they are aware of their responsibilities and expectations.

Insurance—Your congregation's insurance may already provide adequate coverage for service activities away from the church. Investigate to be clear about the responsibilities of the congregation. If the youth are serving in an existing agency (hospital, day-care center) or as part of a national program, these organizations may have insurance that covers volunteers.

Parental Permission—The main value of permission slips is that they are proof that parents and teenagers were aware of any dangers (as long as you make the issues explicit) and that they have consented to the participation—and thus assumed the risks inherent in the project. According to *Education Week,* parental permission slips should include:
- the place where you'll be going and working;
- the type of transportation;
- for trips, the time, date, and place of departure and return; for local projects, the date and time when they occur;
- the project's objectives;
- what young people need to bring.[7]

(Though several youth-ministry books recommend that parents sign waivers of liability, service-learning experts caution that this approach is not advisable, since they are unenforceable and thus give a false sense of security. Furthermore, even if such an approach were legally useful, it is not ethical to try to absolve yourself of liability in cases of negligence.[8] Consult a lawyer about what best fits your needs.)

Supervision and Preparation—No amount of paperwork can protect you from lawsuits if the plaintiffs can prove negligence was the cause of injury. Thus, it is important to document all steps you've taken to assure reasonable safety. These might include:
- master charts that show how young people are being monitored at a work site;
- emergency training for responsible adult and youth leaders;
- adequate adult supervision.

Attract Youth to Volunteer

A successful service-learning project assumes that you will have young people who are interested and involved. Yet, at least at first, you may need to make extra efforts to attract young people to service.

If you've planned and designed your project well, you already have done many things that will make it appealing. For example, if your group has little service experience, a short, low-commitment project will be less daunting, but a more mature, active group will want more. Now what can you do to get young people's attention and involvement?

If possible, have a project in place before recruiting participants beyond the leadership team. "People of all ages are more likely to respond to a request to do some specific task, and nothing will dampen the spirit of a group of volunteers more thoroughly than a long delay between their offer to help and the chance to begin," advise service-learning experts Dan Conrad and Diane Hedin.[9]

Design a strong appeal. Conrad and Hedin suggest that good appeals . . .

. . . are as concrete and specific as possible about the type of work to be done;

. . . convey that service can be enjoyable, not dull and dreary;

. . . stress the challenge and satisfaction of taking and completing a tough job.

"Few young people will be scared off by a significant challenge," they say, "particularly if it is also made clear that they will have ample help and support in facing it."[10]

Build on an interest such as music, sports, or a career. Help young people find ways to contribute by using their special talents or skills. For example, have an artistic teenager volunteer to teach art to young children.

Mike Nygren, of Ginghamsburg United Methodist Church in Tipp City, Ohio, tells about Josh, one of his group members. The group wanted to build a jungle gym for an orphanage in Jamaica, where they had been on a work camp and found no recreational facilities. Knowing Josh's interest in woodworking, Nygren asked him to design and make a small model of the project, which they could use in fund-raising. They planned to "sell" each board in the structure to church members for $10.

As it turned out, Josh spent innumerable hours in his tool shed through the summer, building a detailed scale model of the jungle gym—a model that raised more than $1,000! The next January, Josh oversaw construction of the actual structure in Jamaica.[11]

Make the service tangible. Whether your project is down the block or around the world, try to make it tangible to young people. Hang maps and pictures in the youth room, serve food that reflects the culture, play appropriate music, show videos of the type of work. If the site is local, take a field trip during a regular meeting time; walk around the area and talk to a few people. Or invite people from the community to come to your church to talk about their life and experiences.

Have the youth invite their friends. An Independent Sector study asked teenage volunteers how they first learned about and decided to take part in this activity. The highest category was "asked by someone" (41%), followed by "through participation in an organization or group" (31%) and "had a family member or friend in the activity or benefiting from the activity" (31%). Similarly, when asked who asked them to volunteer, teen volunteers said "a friend" (47%), "a teacher or other school personnel" (31%), "a family member or other relative" (31%), and "someone at church or synagogue" (22%).[12]

Publicize the activity. Don't assume that young people will know about your service activity. Advertisers remind us that people need to see something at least three times before it registers. Use all the techniques available to catch young people's attention.

As part of its confirmation program, Our Father Lutheran Church in Denver, Colorado, requires service in the congregation within the two years of the program, says Margaret Hinchey, who works with the youth. On the first night of confirmation instruction, the church holds a "Confirmation Service Opportunity Fair," where the young people can circulate among booths to decide what kind of service they want to provide. They sign up on commitment sheets and are given information sheets about expectations and times of service.

Whet their appetite for service with field trips and other adventures that will expose them to needs and issues in nonthreatening ways.[13] Use video, simulations, and other learning approaches to build interest. (See page 113 for some suggested resources.)

Target broadly. Seek to avoid the trap of having a service-learning project or program geared solely to one part of the youth group. Design the program to include male and female, good students and poor, older and younger, model citizens and renegades.

Start young. The same Independent Sector study of teenagers mentioned earlier found at least one factor that distinguishes volunteers from non-volunteers: They volunteered as children (younger than age 11). Among the teenagers who reported volunteering as children, 84 percent currently volunteer. This childhood service experience is a more powerful predictor than belonging to a youth group as a child.[14]

Prepare Youth to Serve

Some of the common problems that occur in service projects result because young people have not been adequately prepared. They haven't thought about issues of poverty. They haven't examined their own faith commitment. They haven't practiced the skills they need to succeed in their assignments. They have not been introduced to what they might see, hear, smell, feel, or encounter. Then they "hit the ground running," only to be embarrassed, frustrated, or bored—or to embarrass those they have come to serve. This section briefly highlights some of the orientation and training issues that make service-learning successful.

Match each youth with assignments. Whether you're offering one single project or a variety of opportunities, find ways to match individual young people with appropriate roles in those projects. Be aware not only of the young person's needs, developmental stage, and skills, but also of areas in which the young person wants or needs stimulation, growth, and stretching.

Young people can fill many different roles in a service-learning project. Depending on what you're doing, these can include: organizing a specific aspect of the project, record-keeping, public relations, supply coordination, fund-raising coordination, photography, making phone calls, writing letters and thank-you notes, and participating in the actual work force.

Train in skills and problem-solving. Once again, the specific type of training and skills will depend upon the nature of your service-learning project. If, for example, you're rebuilding homes, you may want to train in basic carpentry—which could become part of a regularly scheduled youth program. If, however, you're launching a peer-ministry program or a hotline for other teenagers, you'll want to provide several weeks of intensive training in helping skills.[15] Furthermore, if you work with community agencies, they may require (and provide) specific training.

Some congregations find it useful to establish short-term "prerequisites" for participating in more intensive work camps and mission trips. These lower-commitment projects are a way to practice skills and begin to think about the issues that will arise in the projects with greater commitment. For example, the youth at Seventh and James Baptist Church in Waco, Texas, must complete at least twelve hours of service in the community before attending the summer mission trip. They work at the local Habitat for Humanity project, learning skills they will need during the summer. In fact, says youth worker Beverly CrowTipton, each must pass a "worker's test" to be sure they are "prepared for what they're going to do."

Begin forming relationships with community residents. If your project involves direct contact with people outside the young people's normal relationships (the elderly, young children, other nationalities, different income levels, etc.), it can be valuable to have them begin to form relationships before the service-learning experience begins. You might, for example, have them correspond with residents of the nursing home where you'll be working. When the young people arrive to begin their work, they will already have had some contact on which to build relationships.

Address key issues. Beyond the specific skills needed for service are the new perspectives and values that need to begin forming. It can often be effective to begin exploring some of the deeper issues surrounding service. This can be done through simulations, Bible study, short-term projects, research, and other information-gathering ways. (The resource listing at the end of this book includes some curriculum that can be useful here.) Some of the issues that might be addressed include:

- True Servanthood—Because people traditionally think of helping others in terms of "me reaching down to pull you up," young servants need to learn that both parties are giving and receiving in service-learning.
- Fears and Prejudices—Young people need to confront some of the fears and prejudices that are inevitable when you serve across diverse populations.
- World Issues—Virtually any service you undertake has complex issues attached to it, whether they are hunger, justice, the environment, abuse, or violence. Introducing young people to these issues in advance will trigger their thinking when they get into a service situation.
- Faith and Life—Finally, through Bible study, prayer, and discussion, young people can begin thinking about the connections between the faith they profess and the lives they lead. Those connections will become vivid during the service-learning experience, and this early discussion can be a springboard to significant spiritual growth.

Keep in mind, however, that while each of these issues is important to begin discussing before service-learning begins, it can be difficult for young people to internalize the new perspectives without experiencing them—which is, after all, one reason you're doing service-learning in the first place. How much do we expect the youth to know before they have learned? Thus, though introducing these issues in advance is appropriate, it is even more vital to deal with them during and following the service experience. That need is the focus of chapter 7.

Build relations in the youth group. Use various activities to help the members of the group develop confidence in and feel supported by one another. This sense of group cohesion will make it more likely that young people will take risks, knowing that others will support them, not laugh at them. Dozens of resources are available with these kinds of activities.[16]

Commission youth to serve. Young people need to be reminded that their work is valuable service in the name of Christ. Many congregations find it appropriate to commission youth to service just before the beginning of a project or a trip. Such a commissioning gives public affirmation of the ministry of the young people.

Involve Families in Service Projects

As we noted in chapter 3, families have more influence than anything else on young people's faith. And we also have noted the problems that can arise when parents don't understand the impact of young people's service experiences. Thus it can be quite valuable to have families serve together. You can facilitate this in several ways:

- Have parents serve as sponsors for your projects or trips. This is the most common approach used by youth groups (see chapter 5).
- Plan one-day service projects for families, so that parents and teenagers learn side by side. Gather afterward to talk about the experience and the issues it raised.
- Provide opportunities for families to sponsor refugees or exchange students in their homes. Then all sponsors can get together to talk about their experiences.
- Create a family support network, wherein families in the congregation are available to be "listening ears" or provide temporary assistance to families in crisis or trauma.
- Have families become "eco-teams" to monitor their own impact on the environment and take action to reduce waste. Provide conversation starters that help families talk about why they're doing what they're doing.
- Set up (or join with) a program that allows families to become mentors to young people who may not have access to healthy family models.
- Give families information about becoming foster families for children waiting to be placed in an adoptive family. Create a support group in the church for these families.
- Have a family-life Christian education series in which families come together to talk about life-style issues (simplicity, conflict resolution, compassion, etc.), spend the week practicing what they discussed, then come back together for debriefing.
- Invite families to serve together in ongoing congregational ministries (soup kitchens, homeless shelters, crisis hotlines, home repairs, etc.).
- Ask families to work together to provide—and celebrate together—birthday meals for the homebound.

Serve and Learn

Do what you planned to do. Work hard. Do a good job. Supervise to ensure quality. Do all those task-oriented things.

But keep in mind the learning side of this project while you serve. For your service to translate into learning, you need the youth to be thinking about what they're doing in the midst of the serving. To illustrate that people don't always think about what they're doing, Conrad and Hedin quote from a student's journal: "Today I got to the nursing home at 2:00. Talked to some ladies. Passed out popcorn at the movie. Went home at 4:00." That same entry occurred twice a week, every week, for the six weeks of her service.[17]

To create a climate where learning can occur, follow these tips:

- As an adult leader, avoid solving the problems that arise (and they will arise), but guide the youth in the problem-solving process. If their problem-solving process is ineffective, talk about it and learn from it.
- Don't take over difficult jobs. Do on-the-job training so that the young people themselves learn.
- Monitor safety and intervene when you see it in jeopardy. No amount of learning is worth a serious accident or injury.
- Work alongside the youth as equals and partners. Don't be just the supervisor who gives the orders.
- Show young people how to interact with community residents: how to introduce themselves; how to listen; how to ask questions. Listen to one anothers' stories. Work side by side if other people offer. As Carol Davis Younger, of College Heights Baptist Church in Manhattan, Kansas, challenges: "Pay more attention to eye contact, hugging, and other personal contact."

- Get into the community's culture. Younger recalls being host to a suburban group that visited her inner-city congregation in Louisville, Kentucky. The youth group would work with the poor inner-city children in the morning, then spend the afternoon shopping in the expensive malls. "It was very clear the difference between the 'haves' and the 'have nots'," she recalls. By not becoming absorbed in the culture on the mission trip, the youth group never really felt the impact that service can offer.
- Ask questions and encourage young people to notice things in one another, in the community residents, in the work. Then talk about those things in your reflection time.
- Consider asking the youth to keep journals or notebooks on their experience. This tool is explained in more depth in Figure 14 in chapter 7.
- If you are on an immersion experience such as a work camp or mission trip, you'll want to plan intentional follow-up reflection during the evenings or at other times. Invite local residents to come and talk with your group about life in the community and the cultural heritage of the people with whom you are serving. The reflection framework suggested in chapter 7 would be a valuable resource.
- Recognize the need for relaxation and laughter. Make time to have fun.

Celebrate and Affirm

Whether your effort is a one-time project (teaching vacation church school) or an ongoing ministry (serving Meals on Wheels), make conscious efforts to affirm the youth who serve, and celebrate the progress that occurs—both during and after the service. For this to occur, you need to document progress, then use whatever opportunities may come along to celebrate and affirm. The congregation also would like an opportunity to celebrate as you share . . .
. . . a letter from a grateful service beneficiary;
. . . a story of the impact of service on a young person;
. . . a completed project;
. . . the development of stronger relationships or skills;
. . . the overcoming of a particularly difficult obstacle (like the absence of supplies at the work camp site!);
. . . new faith or vocational commitments among the youth.

You may also want to assign individual group members to be responsible for different forms of documentation of your project: photography, video, interviews with the youth and residents, and so on. In addition, some of the processing and evaluation methods described in chapter 7 can serve as sources for celebration and affirmation.

Build a Diverse Program

To simplify the explanation of a planning process, this chapter has focused on how to identify, plan, and perform a particular service project. While this step-by-step approach is easier to follow, it doesn't adequately capture the challenge of developing a multifaceted, ongoing service-learning program in a congregation. As we've stressed repeatedly, a single service project does not provide lasting growth and change; that growth and change comes as young people experience serving others again and again across time.

Beyond Leaf Raking

A better approach is to develop a service-learning program piece by piece, project by project. As you develop new projects, you may want to balance . . .

. . . short-term and long-term projects;

. . . projects for beginners and projects for more mature servants;

. . . local projects and national or international projects;

. . . projects that interact with different ages (elderly, children);

. . . projects that address different issues (poverty, racism, violence, disasters, environment);

. . . one-to-one projects and group projects;

. . . projects for different developmental levels of youth;

. . . projects that build different types of skills or competencies;

. . . projects that call on different leaders in the youth group;

. . . projects that build on previous projects, stretching youth physically, intellectually, and spiritually.

. . . You get the idea.

Some people may want to start with a grand strategy—one that lays out the scheme of projects for five years. If that is a useful process for you, use it. But it may be more effective to have a less structured and more spontaneous approach, particularly at first.

Try something and see how it goes. Does the short-term project capture young people's imagination and enthusiasm? If so, can it (and should it) spin off into an effective long-term, ongoing project? What did you learn from that project that applies to another?

In short, let experience be your teacher and guide. Reflect regularly about where you are with your projects, where you've come from, where you're going, and how the experiences are changing you, the youth, and the youth group. Be open to the Holy Spirit's leading—of the group or of individuals.

We opened chapter 2 with the story of Ginghamsburg United Methodist Church's all-encompassing youth service program, which consists of after-school programs in the city, summer work camps to build homes, the serving of a Thanksgiving dinner, and much more. But that church's program didn't start out as a grand scheme. In fact, the whole thing started with a rather simple goal of the youth minister, Mike Nygren: to involve young people in some kind of service project once a month. And some of the things they have tried worked.

The youth ministry's after-school program began when a fourteen-year-old girl expressed an interest in doing something to reach urban children. In the summer of 1988, six teenagers when into the Parkside community of Dayton once a week, just to ride bikes and build friendships. Then during that school year, they went into the city for 18 Thursday afternoons, and by spring, 30 teenagers were involved in a more structured program of reading, stories, snacks, and games.

From that beginning, the Clubhouse program has grown to eight sites, where young people go 120 days a year, operating in rented facilities. The program has a structured curriculum which includes tutoring, skills and hobbies, and spiritual growth. Now the model is being replicated in other communities, where the young people are living while they go to college![18]

Recycle the Learning Cycle

Not only does the Ginghamsburg program illustrate how to build on your successes, it also shows how one experience can grow out of another in an ongoing cycle. Individual service projects can be energizing and rewarding. However, true results come as

projects build upon projects, and as projects and relationships mature. This interaction is illustrated by the four steps of the service-learning cycle:
- Concrete experience and observation;
- Reflection on that experience;
- Synthesis and abstract conceptualization;
- Testing of new concepts in new situations.

Inherent in the model is the ongoing opportunity to have new experiences that build on the previous experience and growth.

For too many youth groups and congregations, however, community service is characterized by an effort here and an effort there. For some, this means trying a new project every month or so. For others, it means deciding each year where to go on an adventurous work camp or mission trip. And if a group does undertake an ongoing project, it may soon die because the group becomes restless, or the support (including funds) dries up, or a misunderstanding or controversy sours people's enthusiasm.

Thus, efforts need to be made to gain an ongoing commitment to service and to specific ministries. Many of the same factors recommended in project planning are also keys to maintaining support (from both institutions and individuals):

- Build relationships among everyone involved—youth and community residents; youth and the congregation; youth and other youth; the community residents and the congregation. As we know from battlefield stories, people rarely will die for causes (or in this case, projects), but they'll almost always die for a close friend.
- Be sure that the program's goals are clearly linked to the congregation's goals. Be sure people see that the program is a direct expression of the congregation's sense of ministry and purpose.
- Build ownership among everyone involved. The congregation, the youth, and the community residents—all must feel that they have a stake in the project. A strong case can be made that youth-service projects should be supported in part by the church budget (not just by fund-raisers) for this very reason.
- Evaluate and reshape. Constantly check signals with people to see how the project is going. Deal with frustrations and problems as you go along. Learn from mistakes.
- Know when to end particular projects. Celebrate what happened. Give closure. And inspire people for the next opportunity. Don't let a project just fizzle out.

Be Patient

Kate McPherson puts it this way:

When we have a vision or sense of urgency about an issue, we tend to want to see it happen now. We don't very often have faith in the ebb and flow. We barely plant the flowers and then we keep pulling them up to see if they are growing. Instead, we need to allow them time to grow, to trust the ebb and flow and changes, and to honor the fact that different people's lives have seasons where they can give more or less attention to such an effort. If you have a commitment, make sure that you see how to integrate that commitment into your own quality of life so that you too can sustain it over time. Constant, steady pressure has more overall force and effect than an occasional, frantic shove.[19]

6 LEADERSHIP FOR SERVICE-LEARNING

As educators, we often do *for* youth, and, in the process, we do *to* them. As a result, the classroom culture frequently becomes one where teachers feel they need to entertain students or coerce them through rewards and instructional techniques. Then we wonder why students are not appreciative and involved.[1]

Sound familiar? Just substitute a few words, and the quote fits all too perfectly into many youth ministries. Adults (or sometimes just the youth directors) run themselves ragged organizing one event after another, teaching classes, leading programs, organizing fund-raisers, and doing anything else they can think of to keep the youth interested and, even more important, on the rolls.

The service-learning model will be effective only if this pattern is broken and leadership roles are redefined. Otherwise, young people may complete the projects and even grow in faith, but they will not develop the sense of accomplishment, the skills, and the ownership that service-learning has the potential to offer.

This is not to say, however, that one can simply tell the youth, "You're in charge; let us know how it goes." Several years ago, in *Youth Ministry: A New Team Approach,* Ginny Ward Holderness told of her initial enthusiasm upon hearing that one youth group was run totally by the young people.

But on further investigation, she learned that each young person signed up at the beginning of the year to be responsible for one Sunday night program during the year. The young people were to invite adults to come and talk to the youth group about something of which they were knowledgeable. "Often there was no program," she writes. "Either the designated young person forgot or could not find anybody. Volleyball became the program. This is not youth leadership."[2]

What's important then, is to redefine roles for the adults and the youth in ways that empower young people in appropriate ways. This chapter suggests appropriate roles for adults and youth in service-learning.[3]

Roles for Youth

Because one of the objectives of service-learning is to empower the youth by nurturing responsibility and leadership, it only makes sense that they take leading roles in planning and implementation. Furthermore, young people express interest in leadership in the church. According to Search Institute's Effective Christian Education study, there is a core of young people interested in a variety of issues that relate to leadership—and issues that leadership can nurture. For example, among youth in Protestant churches . . .

. . . 65 percent are interested in gaining a sense of purpose in life;

. . . 61 percent are interested in "discovering what is special about me";

. . . 59 percent are interested in learning how to make choices and decisions;

. . . 55 percent are interested in developing leadership skills;

. . . 55 percent are interested in learning how they can make a difference in the world;

. . . 53 percent are interested in learning how to apply their faith to daily decisions;

. . . 32 percent are interested in learning about jobs and careers through which they can express their Christian faith.[4]

Beyond Leaf Raking

McPherson suggests that young people can be involved in service-learning planning in several ways:

- Assess needs in the group, congregation, community, nation, and world by conducting surveys, doing interviews, and reading. This gives them ownership in the chosen project.
- Decide how what's being learned in debriefing and reflection can benefit others in the community and world.
- Identify talents, gifts, and resources to be used.
- Develop their own sense of vision for the future.
- Help coordinate logistics, recruit volunteers, and build enthusiasm for the effort.[5]

Nurturing leadership is a key challenge for Zion Baptist Church, on the north side of Minneapolis. The predominantly African American congregation had difficulty keeping the strong leaders among their youth involved in the community. If they had skills and ambition, they would leave the community as soon as they could. "The most capable leadership gets syphoned off," reports youth worker Philip Hannam. And the church wasn't challenging them to grow.

To address these parallel issues, the congregation established an intensive summer program designed specifically to challenge and involve the most capable leaders. Each year, eight to ten of the youth would commit ten to twelve weeks of their summer to the Servant Leadership Project. During that time, they undertook a different type of service every week—in the neighborhood, in the city, in another city, and overseas.

The program aimed at helping teens see that "their faith is important now. . . . They can make a difference now," Hannam says. In addition, the program helped young people examine their values and sense of vocation. What is their vision for life? How will they use the gifts that God has given them to serve? "We were after helping kids develop a vision of Christian mission," he explains.

The program was successful, Hannam believes, when it "put kids back into significant roles that they should have had anyway." He notes that African American youth face numerous challenges in their lives. "Faith has to be a resource in the face of those problems," he says, "or it will become irrelevant." By nurturing young people's leadership skills, the program was able to build youth's ownership in the community.

When seeking to develop leadership skills through service-learning, examine projects and the roles within projects, based on the level of responsibility required. For example, if your group doesn't have mature leaders, you would start with projects that require less responsibility. These would have clearly defined duties, skills, and expectations, with little flexibility or independent judgment required. (These kinds of activities are most appropriate also for elementary students.)

But as your young people experience, reflect, and mature, they can be given more responsibility with less supervision. And, over time, they can become responsible for developing projects and setting policy. Figure 11 shows how these stages build on each other.[6]

One of the challenges, of course, is having advanced leaders and beginning learners work together without friction or feeling threatened. If this proves to be an obstacle, you may need to offer a variety of service projects to meet the different needs and different levels. However, a more exciting possibility is to encourage those who are more skilled to teach, lead, or mentor those with less experience or maturity.

(Note: It is rare for high school students to progress through all five levels of leadership; generally, adults play key roles in the two highest leadership levels.)

Figure 11
Levels of Leadership Development

Level	Characteristics of Tasks	SampleTasks	Leadership Skills Youth Might Learn	Names of Youth
1. Beginning leadership	• Work under close supervision • Clearly defined tasks • Limited options for exercising judgment	• Supervise tutoring • Lead children's classes with established curriculum • Lead recreation in a nursing home	• How to meet schedules and keep commitments • See the importance of service • Understand a need in the community	
2. Intermediate leadership	• Less direct supervision • Some opportunity for independent judgment	• Gathering and assessing information on community needs • Do publicity and recruiting for projects	• How to apply knowledge to a situation • Build confidence in personal skills • Greater problem-solving skills • Understand the residents' viewpoint	
3. Experienced leadership	• Independent judgments necessary • Some supervisory responsibility	• Peer counseling • Organizing specific projects	• Problem-solving skills • The importance of self-initiative • Enable people to help themselves • Role of leadership • Interpersonal and analytical skills	
4. Project leadership	• Advisory and supervisory responsibilities • Independent applying policy	• Developing projects based on community needs	• Skill in translating goals into reality • Understanding relationship between individuals and institutions	
5. Program leadership	• High leadership and management responsibility • Goal and budget-setting with other managers	• Developing and administering a service-learning program	• Confidence in functioning autonomously • Ability to inspire value of service-learning in others	

The Role of Community Members

"We minister *with* people, not *for* them," writes Carl Dudley, in *Basic Steps Toward Community Ministry.* He continues:

> When we do ministry for people, we reduce them to objects. "They" and "we" are different. . . . With our resources we are powerful, and with their needs they are weak. As the providers of ministry, we are the decision makers, and they are the recipients. Sharing ministry with people requires more effort.[7]

The only way to avoid this pitfall is to consider and treat community members as partners in the designing and planning of your service-learning program. Such a perspective is quite difficult to foster, because too often the word service connotes an unequal relationship. "I would argue," writes Nadinne Cruz, "that the possibility of mutuality of interests and needs implied in the concept of reciprocal learning could be more easily realized if it were not tied to any notion of service."[8]

We are not ready to discard the notion of Christian service as inappropriate and irredeemable. However, Cruz's caution is one to take seriously in planning service-learning efforts. Furthermore, because any partnerships between diverse groups is difficult, shared leadership clearly complicates the ministry. But the difficulties involved in shared leadership only heighten the need for such an approach. As Dudley writes, "We make the effort to share ministry across these boundaries because we believe that all people are equal in the forgiving love of God. The purpose of our ministry is to share the empowering grace of God, not to invent new forms of dependency."[9]

How does a youth service-learning effort take seriously this call? Several strategies can contribute:

Listen to the community residents—in person, in surveys, in interviews and focus groups. Include them in your planning and project development.

Early on, share concerns, strengths, and visions. What are community members most worried about? What strengths do they see in their community? What vision do they have for their community? Then, how can your youth group be a partner in bringing that vision to reality?

Include residents on your planning team. If they worry about being unheard in the larger group, consider forming a community council (made up primarily of community residents) to assist in designing and monitoring your ministry.

If you sign up with an existing ministry or program (such as a work camp), *be sure that the program planners have taken seriously the perspectives and priorities of community residents.*

Include community members in the work teams. This can be particularly effective in ongoing ministries, where people who have benefited in the past become significant contributors to the work. This could include tutoring, home repair, leading children's recreation, and so on.

Include community residents in the processing and debriefing. Dave Carver of Twelve Corners Presbyterian Church in Rochester, New York, recalls a mission trip his group took to inner-city Philadelphia. One afternoon during free time, the youth group started a pick-up basketball game. As the teams formed, it became a match between the youth group and the community youth. When the youth group started winning by a large margin, the community team began to play more roughly, until one of the youth-group girls was pushed down and slightly injured.

That night at the debriefing, the group was seething. "Here, we came down to help these people, and they can't even play fair," one member said, and the others nodded in agreement. Then a teenager from the community, who had been listening silently, broke in: "So you guys think you're better than us."

Carver says that the confrontation was tense and intense. But the group worked through the issues together with the neighborhood teenager. Everyone learned more about what it meant to be a servant and a partner.

Get feedback. As your project progresses, check with the community residents about how it's going. Do they feel used? Or do they feel more empowered? Adjust your work and your debriefing accordingly.

Enjoy fellowship and play together. Have a joint picnic to launch your service. Listen to each other's music during the project. Take a break for a game—perhaps a traditional game from the community you're serving, which community members can teach.

In calling for community residents to be active partners in leadership, we recognize how awkward and difficult it can be because of different worldviews, different values, different histories, and different places in life. But, as Dudley concludes, "Your ministry will be stronger if you empower the recipients and affirm the equality of all participants in building a better community, under God. The process of ministry is an important part of its product."[10]

The Staff Person Responsible for Youth Ministry

Often this staff person is expected to be the leader, planner, implementer, and scapegoat for youth service projects. A service-learning approach suggests another model, in which the Christian education director or youth director has an important role, but with limitations.

Service-learning literature suggests that the staff person be the program coordinator. While volunteers can perform the job well, the staff person has advantages of access, visibility, and connection to many different people. The coordinator's role involves . . .

. . . holding up the vision to congregation, staff, youth, and adult volunteers;

. . . developing and facilitating planning times;

. . . coordinating, monitoring, and supporting others who have specific responsibilities;

. . . finding and sharing resources that would be helpful in various aspects of the effort;

. . . coordinating or leading training for adult volunteers and youth leaders;

. . . creating support structures in the congregation for service-learning.

Though these roles are more narrowly defined than "Run the service projects," they are still significant commitments. In many ways, the coordinator must understand and be in touch with all aspects of the ministry. This may sometimes take more work than just doing it yourself. But in the process of coordinating and coaching, you not only accomplish the project at hand, but you equip young people and empower them to make a difference.

The Adult Volunteers

Other adults also have roles in a service-learning program, though, once again, they may not be responsible for the same things the youth-group sponsors typically do. Even more important, though, they need a new perspective on youth. "Adults need to see young people as a resource, and we don't always," says Karen McKinney of the National Youth Leadership Council. "They don't have to wait to grow up. They can do it now. . . . It's not just a potential, it's an 'already'."

Furthermore, adults may need new skills for some of the roles they have traditionally filled. Here are some of the possible roles the adults can fill in a service-learning effort.

- Coordinate an individual project within a larger service-learning program. In these cases, they would fulfill the coordinator's role (above) in the specific project.
- Assist the youth in planning and carrying out their activities.
- Be a role model as a participant in the service and learning process.
- Monitor progress and give feedback.
- Provide transportation and supervision for the youth, to assure safety, minimize risk, and deal with emergencies.
- Facilitate debriefing (unless the youth have been adequately trained in processing and debriefing). Since many adults have never learned facilitating skills, this role may require training and practice.
- Be a consultant and guide as young people plan and lead projects.
- Serve as mentors to teenagers involved in individual service projects or in projects where they learn job and leadership skills.
- Encourage positive and supportive relationships among the youth, particularly as the group broadens and becomes more diverse.
- Be an advocate for and supporter of service-learning in the congregation.
- Use personal connections and resources to identify service partners in the community.
- Hold high expectations of the youth, affirm them, and support them through failure.

To fill these roles, adults may need to learn new skills. Instead of skills in speaking or presenting, they need group-process skills that will enable them to elicit new understanding, process information, handle sensitive issues, and affirm each person's uniquenesses. Rather than knowing a lot of information about a particular subject, adults need to know how to obtain information from people, places, and resources, so that they can direct young people in their learning. In short, adults take new roles as supporters, guides, and mentors. As researchers at the Northwest Regional Educational Library state, "The instructor functions as a facilitator of learning, rather than primarily as a dispenser of knowledge."[11]

Most adults need reorientation and training in order to be effective in these roles, unfamiliar to many in the church. Since many have not experienced this approach, reorienting can be difficult. In extensive research on staff development, Bruce Joyce and Beverly Showers found that several factors need to be in place in order for teachers and other adult leaders to actually change their approaches: (1) practice (they need to actually do it); (2) on-site coaching (they need someone to watch, critique, and give feedback); (3) and collegial support.

They found, for example, that if teachers hear only the theory (why service-learning is important), only 5 percent of teachers can apply that knowledge to their teaching. However, if, in *addition* to the theory (not in *place* of it), the teachers also receive experience and on-site coaching, as many as 80 to 95 percent could apply their learning.[12]

The Parents

Parents can be your greatest allies or your greatest headaches in a service-learning program. Let's look briefly at both possibilities, starting with the allies. Parents are important partners for youth service efforts because they . . .
. . . affirm young people's involvement in service;
. . . sometimes provide transportation and funding for their children's participation;
. . . help young people process their experiences;
. . . permit their children to be involved in the projects;
. . . volunteer to serve as adult sponsors and mentors.

Yet parents don't always fill these roles, making them more like headaches than allies. Why does this happen?

First, parents may not recognize the benefit and impact of serving. Maybe they themselves have seldom or never volunteered. Maybe they had bad volunteering experiences. One of the greatest frustrations when young people return from a service project is to have authentic change and growth dismissed by their parents.

Lack of parental support also can arise when parents have significant concerns about the safety and well-being of their children. They may worry about physical safety, about children being exploited by voluntary service, or about a child failing.

Finally, parents may become roadblocks to your efforts if they feel left out of the effort. But there are several ways to help parents become allies instead of headaches.

Involve Parents—"Whenever possible," suggests Kate McPherson, "involve parents in planning, implementing, and evaluating service programs. Engaging parents early in the process will not only gain their support, but will model service-oriented behavior for students."[13]

Address Fears—(both valid and invalid). Assure parents—with concrete evidence—that you are doing all you can to assure the safety of the young people. Some of parents' fears may grow out of their own prejudices and misinformation about other countries or cultures. In these cases, seek to educate parents about the differences between real and perceived risks.

Schedule in Family-friendly Ways—It's difficult for families to be supportive of efforts that are continual logistical hassles. Furthermore, parents may become antagonistic if they see their teenagers' service involvement cutting into family time and school time. These needs and concerns are legitimate and should be honored.

Inform Parents—Throughout the planning and implementing process, make sure parents are aware of what is happening, what the goals are, and what is expected of them and their teenagers. In addition to regular communication with parents, one youth minister sends a letter to all the parents on the same day the youth leave for a mission trip. In the letter, he tells parents about what their youth are experiencing and asks them to pray for specific things each day. Finally, he encourages them to support and listen to their teenagers after the trip. For example, he suggests that they set a date with their teenagers to go out for ice cream or dinner, to talk about the event, show pictures, and share the impact of the experience.

Offer Family Service Projects—One of the best ways to help parents understand and support service-learning is to let them experience it.

It should be noted that youth-ministry experts are not united in their call for parental involvement. But we believe it is important to include parents, despite possible difficulties. Service-learning, by definition, breaks down traditional hierarchies and challenges people to move beyond their comfortable boundaries. Avoiding the awkwardness will not make it go away. Furthermore, when problems do arise, these can be processed in debriefing to gain important learning (for both parents and youth) about family relationships.

The Pastor

While the pastor may have little direct involvement in the service-learning effort, he or she has a powerful influence over the program's support and acceptance within the congregation. If the pastor affirms and celebrates the ministry, the congregation is likely to do the same. On the other hand, if the pastor ignores, resists, or sabotages the effort, it will have difficulty gaining wide congregational support. Pastors can support service-learning in the following ways.

- Be actively involved in community service, side by side with others.
- In the pulpit, highlight the gospel imperative for service and the value of service-learning.
- Invite young people to tell the congregation about the impact of their experiences on their faith and life.
- Use personal contacts in the community to facilitate service-learning projects.
- Encourage church members to assist with the service-learning program.
- Invite young people to use the leadership skills they're learning in other areas of church life.
- Advocate for resources for service-learning in the church budget.
- Support training for staff members responsible for the youth ministry.
- Recognize youth achievement through service.
- Commission youth to service as part of worship.
- Use excerpts from youth journals as meditations in the church newsletter or weekly bulletin.

Some pastors may see the potential that service-learning has for all ages, from children to senior citizens. If so, the congregation could embark on a unique journey and experiment in merging Christian education and service in ways that could radically reshape church life. But that possibility is beyond the scope of this book.

7 STRUCTURED REFLECTION: LEARNING THROUGH SERVICE

If anyone in the scriptures had a service-learning experience, it was Jonah. He didn't do what God wanted him to do, and he ended by being thrown off a boat only to be swallowed by a fish. Jonah apparently learned from that experience, so he went to Nineveh to preach (or, for our purposes, to serve).

That, too, was a powerful experience: The whole city repented and worshiped God. Did Jonah learn from that? Yes, and he was fuming mad about it. Why should God be merciful to *those* people? The story goes on until Jonah eventually seems to get the point of God's unlimited grace and love.

Experience can be a good teacher, but it's not an infallible one. Sometimes people (like Jonah) can misinterpret an experience and learn inappropriate lessons that reinforce stereotypes and prejudices, rather than broadening their understanding of the world. As Thomas H. Groome writes in *Christian Religious Education,* "It is often glibly asserted that all experience is educational. But this is not automatically true. Some experiences are miseducational and others are not educational at all because we do not attend deliberately and intentionally to what they could possibly teach us."[1]

Dan Conrad and Diane Hedin make the same point: "To say that experience is a good teacher . . . does not imply that it's easily or automatically so. If it were, we'd all be a lot wiser than we are. It's true that we learn from experience. We may also learn nothing. Or we may, like Mark Twain's cat who learned from sitting on a hot stove lid never to sit again, learn the wrong lesson."[2]

In some ways, the nuts-and-bolts details of planning a service project are the easy part of service-learning. You could call up an agency that needs volunteers, schedule a time for the youth group to serve, announce the project several times, and arrange for transportation. What's difficult, though, is building on that experience so that the young people learn and grow from it. And without this component of critical reflection, many of the claims we make throughout this book for the impact of service are unlikely to occur.

An effective service-learning program depends as much on intentional reflection as on the quality of the activity involved. Yet stories from congregations around the country indicate that few youth service programs have developed strong reflection components. Furthermore, most of the available youth-ministry resources on service and mission projects barely mention reflection, if they mention it at all.

Another significant challenge is to link the service project with our faith and beliefs. Unless intentional creative thinking and planning occur, the service will not touch on deep faith issues or challenge young people to think about and internalize their beliefs.

Thus, this chapter focuses on how to make the reflection component in service-learning effective by offering principles and ideas for encouraging critical reflection. We should note that reflection was addressed also in chapter 6 in the discussions on preparing youth to serve and on reflection during the service project. The principles in this chapter can be used to enhance learning in those contexts as well, though here the focus is more specifically on reflection *after* service.

We have developed the chapter around the "Three Whats" of reflection, borrowed from Kate McPherson. In addition, we have tied the reflection to Thomas Groome's five movements of the shared praxis model of Christian education. But before looking at the "Three Whats," we must first build an environment in which effective reflection can occur.

Creating a Reflection-friendly Climate

Anyone who has taught Sunday school or led a group discussion knows that both the environment and the group climate have tremendous influence on the learning process. Uncomfortable chairs, distracting sounds and sights—all can undercut a focused discussion. And the same is true in debriefing a service project. But there are a number of things you can do to establish a climate in which effective processing and learning can occur.

Create a Hospitable, Warm Environment—"The participants need to feel welcome, at home, and at ease," advises Groome. "They need to believe that their contributions will be valued and taken seriously. In such a hospitable environment people are likely to feel free in expressing themselves, speaking their own words rather than saying what they think the group wants to hear."[3]

Some groups foster this kind of environment by establishing explicit ground rules and expectations. Before trying to debrief experiences, decide together what rules need to be in place in order for everyone to feel comfortable in sharing openly. These might include:
- Everyone participates as he or she is comfortable in doing.
- No put-downs or personal attacks will be made.
- Everyone's experience is valid.
- The leader provides structure, not solutions.
- The group focuses on a positive outcome of the experience.
- No comments will be used against anyone later.
- Everything said in the group will be kept in the group.

When possible, this warm emotional climate should be matched with a warm or comfortable physical climate.

Limit Group Size—Any group of more than twelve will have difficulty in quality reflection and processing. Few people will feel comfortable in opening up to a large group. Besides, there's rarely time in a large group for everyone to express themselves with any depth. Furthermore, a smaller group allows the facilitator to pay attention to each young person's expressions, feelings, and concerns.

If your group is large, break into smaller groups (6 to 8), with a facilitator (trained youth or adult) for each group. Keep the smaller groups together for the entire time so that it isn't necessary to rebuild trust and openness at each stage. To allow for a greater sense of community when the large group meets, it may be helpful to assign each smaller group something to bring from the small-group discussion.

Establish Clear Learning Objectives—The forms or techniques of reflection are not as critical as the goal that is established. As Gerry Ouellette writes, "The list of tools could go on and on, but the goal nearly always remains the same. We reflect to understand where we have been, what we have gained, and where we go from here."[4]

Within that broad goal, however, you may have a variety of specific learning objectives that you hope to accomplish through reflection. Some of the possibilities are outlined below in Figure 12, based on Kate McPherson's suggested outcomes of reflection in service-learning.[5] Use this worksheet to name the specific goals you hope to accomplish through your reflection in whatever categories are more important for your educational purposes. As examples, we've included a possible objective in each category.

Figure 12
Goals of Reflection on Service

By reflecting on our service project, our young people will . . .

Foster lifelong learning skills

Learn to apply their faith to their everyday choices

Develop problem-solving skills

Learn how to talk to people who are different from them

Increase sense of personal power

Discover that God has given them important gifts to use in service to others. Be affirmed in their sense of self-worth. Gain respect from adults

Celebrate and renew

Be renewed in their faith commitment

Foster higher-level thinking

See the connection between their life-style choices and inequities in our world

Reinforce academic skills

Learn how to use a Bible concordance and dictionary to explore the relation of scripture to contemporary issues

Encourage personal growth

See themselves as having leadership skills to share with others

Improve service

Become more effective in providing services for the elderly

Improve the service-learning program

Choose to start a project that addresses the justice issues related to the poverty they saw during the work camp

Foster a Thinking Climate—Critical thinking isn't easy. It involves more than sitting in a circle to answer "How did it make you feel?" For critical reflection to be effective, it must challenge young people to look deep inside themselves at their motivations, values, and beliefs. It tests those assumptions and experiences against the resources of faith (prayer, community, scripture, tradition) and social understanding. That may involve intensive research and study. And it may result in a painful process of self-discovery.

Most young people in the church don't experience this kind of challenge to think. In Search Institute's study of Effective Christian Education, only 42 percent of 7th- through 12th-graders said that their church challenges their thinking, and only 45 percent said their church encourages questions. Little wonder, then, that only 31 percent of the youth said that church is interesting.[6]

In debriefing a service project, the questions you ask (and your responses to the answers) will have a great impact on whether you are nourishing a thinking climate. That's one reason the learning objectives need to be in place. And if you respond to a wild or heretical answer to a question by condemning or lecturing (as opposed to further questions to help young people explore the implications of what they have just articulated), young people will be less likely to express themselves openly or explore the issues thoroughly.

A thinking climate also can be fostered by encouraging young people to pursue their own questions after the session, instead of trying to wrap everything up neatly by answering all the questions. For example, your statement, "I really don't know why poor people sometimes have big cars and eat expensive junk food. How could we find out?" could lead young people into some interesting research and discovery and growth in the weeks ahead.

Become a Keen Observer—"You've got to learn to be keenly aware of what the youth are doing. Otherwise you . . . don't know the questions to ask," says Karen McKinney of National Youth Leadership Council, who has worked in congregation-based youth programs.

She illustrates by describing a situation. Your youth group is going to cook, serve, and share in a meal at a soup kitchen. When you arrive, you discover that another group also has been scheduled, has already cooked the food, and is ready to serve. The shelter director says, "We're really sorry. But since you're here, we really could use your help in cleaning up this kitchen—scrub the walls and stuff." So your group goes to work.

As a leader, you need to begin asking yourself how your group is handling the shift of gears, McKinney says. How are they interacting with the shelter guests? How are they interacting with the other youth group? How are they interacting with one another? What roles and tasks do different group members take? Only then can you ask the right questions: "I heard the comment that you were upset about not getting to serve. What bothers you about that?" "How was it to sit next to Mr. Jones who is really hungry, and you know you can go home and have a hamburger?"

Match the Reflection Style and the Questions to Each Person's Developmental Level—The reflection abilities of a sixth-grader are quite different from those of a twelfth-grader. While younger youth will not be able to think abstractly, the older youth will. As Groome writes, "This means that I cannot ask my fourth-graders to reflect on the presence of hatred and animosity among humankind or on the call to universal love . . . but I can ask them 'Why do you fight with your sister?' or 'How did you feel when you beat up your little brother?'"

Groome suggests that critical reflection among younger youth (in the concrete operational stage of Piaget's developmental theory) needs to focus on helping them "comprehend the reasons for and consequences of present action. If education fails to promote such reflection at the stage of concrete operations, it is far less likely that critical reflection in anything like its fullness will be exercised later."[7] At the same time, the younger youth should also be stretched beyond their current thinking patterns, particularly by the time they reach early adolescence.

Leading the younger youth in reflection can be a challenge for other reasons as well. Barbara Varenhorst, a pioneer in peer counseling and peer ministry, writes that not only do younger youth think concretely, but they also have a limited vocabulary and tend to be self-conscious. "Junior-highers' form of looking inward most often is negative," she writes. "They are sure other kids are watching and criticizing them. They don't want to do or say anything that will make others laugh or put them down."[8] This becomes a significant challenge when trying to persuade them to open up and reflect honestly on their service experiences. Varenhorst suggests six principles that help in discussions with junior-highers:

- Have a clear purpose for the discussion.
- Make the discussion meaningful and relevant.
- Use specific, understandable questions.
- Respond to comments respectfully and seriously.
- Encourage young people to respond to one another, so that it's not just a dialogue between you and each individual.
- Pace the discussion to fit with younger youths' limited attention span.

Older youth also need a supportive, meaningful environment for discussion. However, they can think in more abstract terms and should be challenged to do so, as they generalize from their own experiences during the reflection process.

Ask the Right Kind of Opening Question—Your opening question will set the stage for the entire reflection process. If you ask the wrong one, it can be taken as an attack that makes young people think they need to justify what they did. Or it can lead them quickly to talk about an abstract concept or something they are "supposed" to say or believe. As we will see below, the opening question should call young people to explore and own their experience, not defend it.

Be a Fellow Pilgrim, Not an Expert—We've already hinted at this point several times, but it bears repeating. As a facilitator of learning, your role is not to give the information, but to provide a structure that leads youth to their own discoveries. Assuming you also participated in the service, share your own experiences, insights, and struggles as a fellow Christian pilgrim.

The Reflection Process

With these foundational issues in mind, we turn now to the steps in a reflection process. It may be helpful here to note the role played by reflection in the overall experiential-learning cycle. Essentially, reflection focuses particularly on the elements of "observation," "meaning," and "application" (see Figure 2). It also parallels the five movements of Thomas Groome's shared praxis approach, which he describes as "a group of Christians sharing in dialogue their critical reflection on present action in light of the Christian story and its vision toward the end of lived Christian faith."[9]

There are essentially three "whats" in reflection, which generally occur sequentially.[10] Critical reflection moves from experience (What?), to meaning (So What?), and back to experience (Now What?). However, these elements should not be construed as a rigid plan, but rather as a style or attitude. Let's now look at each stage and how to make each one most effective.

Figure 13
Service/Learning and Learning Styles

One of the values of the service-learning cycle (of which the reflection described in this chapter is a vital component) is that it addresses the needs of young people with different learning styles. David Kolb, whose learning cycle is widely used in service-learning circles, shows how different people's learning styles correspond with the four stages of the experiential-education learning cycle.

In reality, different people learn more in different stages of the cycle. However, by including all the stages, every student, at some point, has an opportunity to learn in the most comfortable style for him or her. Here are Kolb's four stages, with a brief description of the type of person who learns best at each stage.[11]

Concrete Experience—Youths who immediately sense the mood of a group, or immediately start dancing when they hear music they appreciate, learn best through concrete experience.

Reflective Observation—Young people who learn best in this stage are the ones who sit back and absorb experiences, beginning to make sense of things by watching intently and reflecting on their meaning.

Abstract Conceptualization—These learners are the young people who build models and concepts to explain things. They enjoy learning theories.

Active Experimentation—Someone who quickly gets involved with people to try out new (even risky) ideas does best at this stage.

What?

You've just returned to the church from an afternoon during which six youth-group members led activities and played games with children at a nearby after-school program. You ordered pizza in advance, and the group is sitting down to enjoy the pepperoni and anchovies (yeah, right!). You say grace, and the youths start digging in.

Before anyone says more than, "This looks great! I'm starved," you pop the question: "Well, guys, how do you feel about our experience today?"

Everyone stops eating, but nobody talks. Finally, one shrugs and mutters, "Okay, I guess." And after a bit of probing, you conclude that maybe the teenagers didn't get as much out of the experience as you had hoped.

Being tenacious, you take another group back to work at the center the next week. Another pizza, another opportunity to talk. This time, though, you ask them to tell some stories from the afternoon. Sara tells about a goofy six-year-old who kept making faces at her. Don tells about all the trouble he had getting a game started. And soon the pizza is mixing well with the laughter and groans of memories.

The difference between the two incidents concerns more than a different group of teenagers. The difference is that the first time, you started with the most difficult question. You asked the young people to think critically about an experience they hadn't really named or internalized yet.

Movement 1: Look at Life—The first step in processing a service experience is to focus on what actually happened. In Groome's model, this would be the first movement in which the participants talk about their experience. "The important task," Groome

91

advises, "is to elicit a personal statement on present action rather than a statement of *theoria* based on what 'they say.' "[12]

Some may ask why bother talking about these kinds of things. After all, "Everybody was there; we know what happened." But when we skip this stage, we don't allow people to synthesize, organize, and internalize the experience. Experiential educators note that there is a hierarchy of thinking levels, beginning with knowledge (memory, information recall) and comprehension (being able to explain that knowledge).

These first two levels of thought must be in place before we move on to application (simply using the knowledge correctly), analysis (breaking pieces apart to discover connections, causes, and motives), synthesis (putting pieces back together for understanding), and evaluation (forming a judgment or opinion).[13] For instance, in the illustration above, when you jumped quickly to analysis in that first week, the youths had not had time to go through the first four stages.

While it isn't necessary to ask robotic questions at each stage, it is important to recognize where the young people are, so that you can start at the right level. The first question in the example might have been appropriate if your group had been sharing stories and talking at length about the experience as you were returning to the church.

There are, of course, many ways for the youth to process the "What" stage. Here are some, borrowed in part from Kate McPherson.[14]

- Ask each person to summarize the experience in one sentence or word.
- Ask one person to recount the event, but if someone thinks that person has missed something, he or she says "Hold it!" and continues the story where the last person left off.
- They could tell the story in the present tense—as if they were actually reliving the experience.
- Show pictures (or videos) of the experience and talk about it.
- Ask them to read excerpts from their own journals (only if the group's trust level is already high).
- Each youth could choose one thing to focus on during the project (such as one task or one person), and then describe that thing or person to the rest of the group.
- Create an impromptu skit to reenact what happened.
- Write a letter to a friend or parent describing the experience.
- Draw pictures from the experience.
- Use modeling dough to recreate something significant from the experience.

Clearly, these ideas have a broad range of complexity. A good rule of thumb may be that the longer between your actual service and the debriefing, the more complex or involved the "What" stage should be, since it will be more difficult for the youth to recollect the memories.

So What?

Once young people have named their experience, they can begin to interpret it. What impact did the service experience have? What difference did it make? Why do we do what we do? At this stage—the heart of critical reflection—they think about what they learned from the experience, exploring its impact on themselves and their faith, on the service recipients, on the community, and on the group.

This stage encompasses three "movements" in Groome's Christian education model (2, 3, and 4), which are particularly helpful in understanding how to guide young people through this stage of critical reflection.

Figure 14
Reflecting Through Journaling

Service-learning educators use a number of tools to help the youth reflect on their experience. Most continually find journaling (or keeping a diary or notebook) to be particularly effective because it is personal, and it allows young people to record their thoughts in the midst of the service, not just afterward.

As a journaling guide for college students explains, "[It] causes you to think about your experiences and can help give you insight into what you are experiencing and how you are feeling about it. It can also give you a useful record of your service and learning."[15]

Journaling is a especially effective when young people are involved in an ongoing ministry which they return to week after week, or when they go on an immersion experience (mission trip, work camp, or urban plunge). In these cases, you may want to make journaling part of your suggested time for personal devotion.

Helping young people journal effectively involves more than just giving them a blank notebook. Here are some options:

- As a leadership team, write a series of process questions in the sequence described in this chapter (maybe one or two per stage), and suggest that students answer the questions after each day of service.
- Give them a list of questions to help answer their plea, "What should I write in my journal?" These might include: What was the best thing that happened to you today? How did it make you feel? How have you changed or grown since you began this project? What are some of the advantages and disadvantages that people in this community have? If Jesus had been in our work crew today, what might he have said?
- Suggest a structure for the journal (or give out pre-printed pages). Space might be given for an objective account of the day's events, feelings about the events, reflection on what they learned, and what actions they'll take next time, based on what happened that day.
- You may have a rotating group of young people with responsibility for a program (such as serving in a soup kitchen, or staffing a homeless shelter or an after-school program.) In these cases, you might find a group diary or journal to be an effective way to create a sense of shared experience as young people read the others' experiences and add their own to the collective memory.

Movement 2: Reflect on Life. The second movement seeks to help the youth understand why we do what we do, and what our hopes are in doing it. Groome often introduces his movement by asking people why they expressed what they did during the first movement. For example, you might say, "José, you really seemed to notice how much of the garbage we collected consisted of beer cans. What made that particularly important to you?" Or, "Why was it so hard for us to relate to the guests in the soup kitchen?"

In these ways, young people begin connecting the service experience with their own values, perspectives, and histories. This self-discovery can be painful and awkward. While all should be invited to speak, no one should be forced. As Groome advises, "We should not assume, however, that the silent ones are not participating in the dialogue. My own experience has been that when I am truly listening, I find myself entering into dialogue within myself with each person who speaks."[16]

Beverly CroweTipton of Seventh and James Baptist Church in Waco, Texas, tells about one group member who was rough and difficult. One day while working on a

Habitat for Humanity house in town, he volunteered to insulate the crawl space under the house—a difficult and messy job.

That night as they reflected on their service, CroweTipton recalls that the teenager's eyes filled with tears: "All he could think about was that, because of what he had done, someone would be warm next winter." That sharing didn't miraculously change him, but CroweTipton hopes that that one moment of vulnerability, together with other little "moments of grace," can lead to significant change in the young man's life.

Movement 3: Knowing Our Faith. At this stage, the goal is to bring the Christian tradition and call to bear on the young people's service experience. "This is the most obviously [related to teaching] movement in the process," writes Groome. "It is the 'echoing,' the handing down, of what has come to us over our past pilgrimage."[17]

This introduction of the faith story can be done in a number of ways, as long as the presentation is made "in a disclosure rather than a closure way—that is, a way that invites people, bringing their own stories and vision, to reflect upon, grapple with, question, and personally encounter what is being presented. . . . The tradition can give life," Groome suggests, "but dogmatism is barren and arrests the journey toward maturity of faith."[18]

It would be impossible within the confines of this book to explore all the implications of this perspective, and other resources present many helpful models and methods for Bible study with youth.[19] Whatever approach is taken, this teaching should be done so that the youth have access to the tradition in ways that enrich and give meaning to their lives.

Though Groome isn't explicit, this movement would also be the stage in which one adds insight from other disciplines or perspectives that give a deeper understanding of the issues involved. Depending on the educational goals, the service project, and the developmental needs of the students, this information could include economic or political theory, information on other cultures, and other relevant information.

CroweTipton recalls a mission trip to San Antonio, where they worked with a variety of agencies that deal with poverty. The youth group would serve breakfast at one place, distribute clothes in another place, serve in yet another soup kitchen, and staff another overnight shelter.

As they moved from location to location, the group members discovered that they were seeing the same faces time and time again. As a group, they discussed the way homeless people were forced to live, roaming from service to service in the community. Adding to the value of the experience, homelessness was the national debate subject that year, and several group members were involved with school debate clubs. CroweTipton was able to build on all the research they had done as the group processed the information. "They came to know more of the cycle of poverty and what a difficult experience it is."

Toward the end of the San Antonio trip, the youth went out for dinner on San Antonio's Riverwalk. There on the benches, they saw some of the same people to whom they had served soup. Once again, the group had an opportunity to talk in depth about the issues surrounding homelessness. They mentioned how differently they viewed these people, now that they knew their names. Weeks later, the youth minister overheard one of the group arguing with a friend about homelessness. In exasperation, the group member had declared, "You don't understand. I know these people!"

It should be noted that, though this kind of information can be presented by a speaker or teacher, young people themselves also can gather and present it. While we rarely ask them to do research or presentations at church, they do it all the time in school—sometimes on far less relevant and interesting topics.

The goal is to give students access to information so that they can draw from its insights to inform their own story. While we want them to search out information, we need not ask them to reinvent theology, political theory, or economics out of their own heads without the wisdom of others.[20]

When this stage of reflection is not thoroughly and adequately undertaken, one risks losing the connection to the faith story and the rich opportunity to help young people connect their life experience to that story. At the same time, if the approach seeks to impose an interpretation and a set of doctrine, it risks backfiring. Groome provocatively notes: "One wonders if the fact that the great majority of people remain at [Fowler's] stage three of faith development [which usually begins at age 11 or 12] is not due, at least in part, to a religious education that taught too much, too soon, too finally, and from the outside of lived experience."[21]

Movement 4: Making the Faith Our Own. The previous movement set the stage for this movement, in which young people's story and vision go into dialogue with the Christian story and vision. The essential question here is, "What does the community's Story mean for . . . our stories, and how do our stories respond to . . . the community Story?"[22]

Now it is time to ask young people to generalize from their own experience, in dialogue with the information presented in the previous movement. What do you think the Bible is telling us about dealing with violence in our city? The goal is for faith (and the other information presented) to inform the young people's service, and for that faith (and the other information) to be appropriated into their lives. The key to making this happen is to pose careful questions that do not elicit "right or wrong" answers, but rather challenge young people to draw from their own understanding.

It also can be useful at this stage to ask what difference the service experience made in the lives of everyone involved. How did you benefit? What did you learn? Did the service empower the recipient? How did the community benefit? Did the group work well together? These kinds of questions bring the group members' own experiences into dialogue with the rest of the wisdom collected (from scripture, etc.), so that they can begin to form a new vision and internalize new understandings.

Now What?

Movement 5: Living Our Faith. Now the young people are ready to ask how the insight and knowledge gained from this process might be helpful in similar or different situations in the future. The answers to their questions can focus on life in general or on the service project in particular. For example, after reflection on a home-repair project, a young person might conclude, "I'm going to write a letter to my congressional representative to push for tax breaks for low-income families." Or the same reflection might lead to: "Next time we work on a house, I'm going to take time to talk with the family— to really find out what life is like for them."

Groome notes that we sometimes have difficulty with this stage. We tend to say, "People need to realize that . . . " or, "The church should . . . ." To overcome this tendency, he encourages participants to begin their remarks with, "I will do . . . " or, "For me this means . . . ."

This is the stage in which people make faith commitments. A commitment can involve a concrete action ("I'll stop driving anywhere I could walk") to a new awareness ("I won't look down on people who are bitter about poverty"). Or someone might say, "I've never thought about this before. I need to think about it some more."

These types of commitments can be elicited in many ways—not just by asking, "What are you going to do now?" Other questions might be more fruitful:

- You seemed disappointed with the way you acted today. What are you going to do differently tomorrow?
- You really seemed to enjoy spending time with the people in the nursing home. How will this experience affect your college or career plans?

McPherson also suggests challenging young people to imagine themselves in a future situation. How would they handle the situation? Have them role play—and come up with at least four different ways to deal with the situation.[23] Encourage them to think of new ways to act and think, based on what they've learned. The more specific they are, the more likely they are to achieve their goals.

Another way to bring closure and commitment is to give young people an opportunity to develop some sort of product that integrates their experience and learning. "It is in giving expression to what we have learned that learning is solidified, clarified, and incorporated into our being," write Conrad and Hedin.[24] They suggest some ways to encourage the youth to express their commitment or new understanding, and we have expanded on these for churches:

- Prepare a tip sheet for others who volunteer later on.
- Develop a skit, drama, or video that expresses what was learned.
- Teach younger children about the experience in a Sunday school class.
- Make a presentation about the experience to the congregation or church council.
- Individually, visit people in the congregation who supported the effort financially, to thank them and let them know what a difference it made in the young person's own life.
- Have a worship service, picnic, or potluck to celebrate the project.
- Write a song or rap about what they learned.
- Publish an article in the church newsletter: "The Top 10 Things We Learned from Our Service Project."
- Create a scrapbook, arranged not by sequence, but by the themes of things they learned through the project.

In addition, you will want to conclude this cycle of the reflection process with evaluation of the project, in order to prepare for the next one (or for continuation of the ongoing project).

A Messy Process

Once again, we have presented a clean, linear sequence that may help you understand how to lead service-learning reflection. In reality, there are few times when a reflection experience will go as smoothly as your notes or sets of questions. "Teachable moments" will emerge in the discussion and take the group into areas you never considered. (Off-track "rabbit chases" also can come up, but that's another issue.) And sometimes the learning process can start because of experiences you never planned.

Dean Feldmeyer tells of taking his group from a wealthy suburban area on a week-long camp in Appalachia to repair a home. Every night the group would talk about the day, and the teenagers became increasingly upset by the homeowner for whom they were working. Each day, the man just sat around in the shade smoking and drinking beer, watching the group work. The teenagers had concluded that the man didn't "deserve" their services.

So the project leaders began to tell the man's story—that he had been disabled and had no workers' compensation; that the mine where he worked had closed down, leaving no jobs in the area. But the teenagers weren't convinced.

Figure 15
Sample Reflection Questions

The following examples of a reflection process show potential questions for the three "Whats" of reflection. These questions need to be adjusted significantly to fit your group, its developmental stage, your learning objectives, and your stage in the process. Futhermore, you may find that an experience, a simulation, or another teaching technique is more effective at some of these stages. What's important to keep in mind is that it is your questions that lead the youth toward greater understanding and commitment.

Direct Experience	The youth spend a spring Saturday digging up gardens and planting seeds with low-income families in their community.	Young people organize a community awareness campaign about child abuse.
What?	• What was the funniest thing that happened to you today? • Describe the family you worked with. What do you know about them? • How is that family's life different from and similar to your family's life?	• What were your roles in this overall campaign? • What was the most rewarding or challenging thing you did? • How did people in the community respond to you in your efforts?
So What? Reflecting on life	• Why was it so hard to talk with some of the families in our community? • Why was it important to you to spend your day doing this?	• Why was _____ so difficult for you in this effort? • What issues did your work make you think about? • What skills or interests did this experience nurture in you?
Knowing our faith	• Have the group read Old Testament passages about gleaning, and talk about the reasons for it in biblical times. • Explore how profit motivates today's farmers and food industries to waste food.	• Examine passages in the prophets that discuss protecting the most vulnerable in society. • Invite a counselor or a recovering victim of abuse to talk with your group about the cycle of abuse.
Making the faith our own	• If that gleaning policy were written today, what do you think it would say? • How can we as individuals and as a group live out the spirit of the gleaning laws in the Old Testament?	• What is the greatest challenge we as Christians face regarding this issue? • What statement, if any, should the church make about this issue?
Now What?	• What is one thing you can begin doing this week that will protect the rights of the least protected in our world? • What can our group do to give low-income families the protection that winnowing was established to give?	• How has this project changed your attitudes toward abuse? • What will you notice now that you didn't notice before? • What can we as a youth group do now to have more impact in this area?

Beyond Leaf Raking

Finally, Feldmeyer started a role-play. He would be the man, and the teenagers could ask him anything they wanted. They started firing away, and he kept responding with excuses and apathy. As the conversation continued, one of the girls broke in: "You guys," she said. "We're treating him like he's broke, and that's not his problem. He's broken!"

For the first time, the group began to understand the true depth of the cycle of poverty and despair. As Feldmeyer concludes, "You can't teach that during church. They've got to get out and experience it."

What he doesn't say is that they might not ever have learned the lesson without his effort in carefully guiding (even tugging) the group to think and reflect in ways that stretched their faith and their understanding of the world.

8 EVALUATING SERVICE-LEARNING EXPERIENCES

To many people in charge of youth-ministry programs, *evaluation* is not a friendly word. It conjures up images of monstrous forms, busy-work, and tedious report-writing. Even worse, many fear that evaluation is a way for superiors to spy on and meddle in programs.

We think of evaluation positively. Done well, it is a helpful tool that can make a significant difference in the life of a service-learning program. And done well, the process of evaluation actually can be enjoyable and generate deep satisfaction.

In the context of congregational service-learning programs, evaluation should have three primary purposes.

- The first is *program improvement*. By taking a careful look at a program and how it has been implemented, one can discover program strengths that should be continued, pinpoint program issues which call for more concerted effort, and develop priorities for program enrichment.
- A second primary aim of evaluation is to document *program outcomes*. By this we mean assessing the impact of the program. Did the group do what it set out to do? What difference did it make? Was the impact as intended, or were there surprises?
- A third function is to provide information for *celebration, interpretation, development,* and *publicity.*

Service-learning outcomes fall into three broad categories: service outcomes, youth outcomes, and congregational outcomes.

Service outcomes refer to the impact of service-learning on the people or issues it was designed to influence. It can include counting the number of people helped or quantifying the amount of help given (e.g., the number of goods collected for a foodshelf; the number of trees planted; the number of people who attended a forum on racial discrimination). Or it can include measures of their satisfaction with the service.

Youth outcomes refer to the impact of service-learning on the participating youth. Did it, for example, influence values or attitudes? Did it build a sense of responsibility or shape a newfound commitment to a vocation of service?

Finally, *congregational outcomes* have to do with the impact of service-learning on congregational dynamics, mission, and programming. Here, one might want to look at how service-learning changed adult perceptions of youth, or whether youth participation in service rubbed off on others, motivating adults in the congregation to begin new service initiatives.

Evaluation also can have a political purpose. Providing information about service outcomes or youth outcomes to one's congregational leadership, for example, could be instrumental in increasing the youth budget or in establishing the need for a youth minister. And such information also could be used to entice new adult volunteers into the youth program, or be used to recruit the youth that have been inactive.

This chapter offers some practical guidelines for conducting useful evaluation in the two areas of program improvement and assessing outcomes. Again, such work should be seen as central—not peripheral—to the task of developing effective service-learning programs. It is recommended that program leaders conduct at least an annual evaluation, following some or all of the suggestions discussed in the next two sections.

Improving Your Program

Beyond Leaf Raking has documented a number of dynamics that enhance the effectiveness of service-learning. These dynamics include assessing community needs, targeting service projects to your youths' activities and interests, establishing program goals, preparing the youth to serve, including parents in the program, building congregational interest in the program, training leaders, providing quality opportunities for the youth to learn from the service, and involving many of the youth in the program.

Figure 16 is designed to help you analyze what you have accomplished in each of these areas, which accomplishments you particularly want to celebrate, which dynamics you want to be sure to hold on to, and where improvement is needed.

How can you best collect information to fill out the worksheets? Much of this can be done in one or several group meetings at the end of a program year, usually in May or June, or soon after a special project. There are two primary groups with whom to hold a year-end conversation. One is the group of youth who participated in service-learning, and the other is the group of adults who helped to shape and/or lead the program.

In some congregations, it will make sense to hold one meeting attended by both groups. In other congregations, one may want to split into two groups. In either case, you might advertise the meeting as an opportunity to discuss "what we did, what we celebrate, and what we can do better."

During the group meetings, try using small-group processes at several points, asking people to pair off, or work in groups of three or five, to discuss one of the questions on the worksheets. It would also help to create large worksheets for each of the topics, so that you can record, for everyone to see, major group conclusions. Following the meeting, transfer the comments to the 8½" x 11" worksheets for a permanent record.

Evaluating Service-Learning Outcomes

This second kind of evaluation—assessing outcomes or impact—can be very time-consuming. And precision about outcomes often demands rigorous scientific methods and heavy time and dollar investments. We suggest a somewhat softer approach, which still is informative and can help to both improve the service-learning program and entice others in the congregation to become excited about it.

Service Outcomes. The task here is to document how much service has been offered. In addition, it is vital that you talk with community residents to assess the service outcomes. Were their needs addressed? Did they feel empowered or used? What would they suggest be done differently? The worksheet in Figure 18 (along with the sample in Figure 17) provides an opportunity to list each of the projects done in the previous year and record the number of people served (or the amount of help given). Furthermore, it is a good idea to note the number of young people involved in the program.

This worksheet becomes an important historical document. Over time, these documents can be compared, to track trends in services provided, or to make summary statements across a number of years. The worksheet should be updated after each service-learning activity.

Figure 16
Program Improvement Evaluation Worksheet

Topic	What did we accomplish?	What should we do again?	How can we improve?
1. Assessing Community Needs (Did we identify service most needed in our community? How accurate was our assessment?)			
2. Assessing Our Youths' Service Interests and Abilities Did we appropriately assess and involve the youth?)			
3. Establishing Program Goals (Did we establish appropriate goals for the program?)			
4. Preparing Youth to Serve (Did we prepare youth for issues faced during service?)			
5. Involving Parent (Did we draw parents into the program?)			
6. Building Congregational Interest (Did we inform leaders and connect to our traditions?)			
7. Training Leaders (Did we help leaders develop necessary skills for conducting a program? Did youth gain leadership skills?			
8. Learning from Service (Did we provide quality opportunities for the youth to reflect on, discuss, and learn from? Did we tie that learning to scripture and our faith heritage?)			
9. Involving Youth (Did the program involve middle-grade and high school students? Boys and girls? Did youth lose interest? What will increase number of participants?)			

Figure 17
Sample Service Outcomes Evaluation Worksheet

Service Project Offered	Project Purposes	Number of People Served and/or Amount of Help Given	Number of Youth Involved		
			Grades 6-8	Grades 9-12	Total
1. Neighborhood beautification	Plant trees on boulevard by the church	28 trees planted; $150 dollars raised through car wash	24	16	40
2. Homeless shelter	Staff foodline for city shelter	Served 650 meals (10 Friday nights x 65 people)	12	15	27
3. Diversity fair	Educate congregation about diversity	160 adults attended	20	18	38

Youth Outcomes. What impact does involvement in service-learning have on youth? If done well and consistently, it could promote positive values, enhance empathy, deepen commitment to service, inhibit negative behaviors, shape a lifelong commitment to service, and deepen faith. One of the best ways to evaluate such outcomes is to collect anecdotes, stories, and personal testimonies. Occasionally during the year, and certainly at the end of the year, assemble the youth for an evening of food, recreation, and conversation. During the conversation, ask them to explain how their participation in service influenced them. For trigger questions, you might ask after initial "What" questions . . .
. . . "What difference did this service program make in your life?"
. . . "What have you learned from this program?"
. . . "Do you do anything differently now because of this experience?"

Be sure to record the comments, type them up, and keep them as part of an evaluation file. You may want to augment or replace the group conversation with some individual interviews.

If you asked the youth to keep a journal of their experiences, ask if they would let you read them. Apply no pressure here, for some journals may be best kept confidential. The journals could be a rich treasure of impact stories and anecdotes. You might consider taking notes on some of the personal transformations and keeping a record of these. Be sure to record anonymously, designating each story with a description such as "boy, age 15," or "girl, age 13." Also leave these notes in the evaluation file.

There are two other sources of recordable anecdotes. Ask adult leaders for the changes they have seen. And assemble a group of parents to gain their perspective on how their children were shaped by service-learning.

Figure 18
Service Outcomes Evaluation Worksheet

Service Project Offered in Last Year	Project Purposes	Number of People Served and/or Amount of Help Given	Number of Youth Involved		
			Grades 6-8	Grades 9-12	Total
1.					
2.					
3.					
4.					
5.					
6.					
7.					
8.					
9.					
10.					

All of what you hear from all these sources may not be positive. Some may tell of disinterest, or boredom, or of feeling powerless to change things. The frequency of these kinds of stories could help to inform program directions for the next year.

Examining Congregational Outcomes

Finally, evidence of congregational change should be recorded. Interviews with adults, pastors, or Christian education teachers could elicit evidence of how the congregation has changed its perception of youth or has become more open to their involvement in congregational life. Simple observation is also useful here. Ask other leaders of the service-learning program to be attentive to congregational impact and ask leaders to share their observations. Record these impressions and add them to the evaluation file.

What use is made of all this evaluation information? The most obvious and important use is to incorporate it into planning. To know "what we have done and how well we did it" is essential background for refining and expanding service-learning.

Less obvious, but potentially important, is the process of communication. The most powerful interpreters are the youth. Have them summarize the achievements of the program and tell their stories to the entire congregational family. Ask some to write articles for the church newsletter, and ask for a spot on the agenda of your church council or similar leadership group.

Service-learning should not be kept a secret. By telling its story, the prospects of generating congregational excitement and support increase.

Special Note to Readers

As you evaluate your program and learn more about conducting effective service-learning in your church, we at Search Institute would like to hear your story. We hope to continue learning in this area as well, so that we may develop additional resources to help congregations in their efforts with youth.

Send descriptions of your programs, newspaper clippings, and other information to:

Eugene C. Roehlkepartain
Search Institute
700 South Third Street, Suite 210
Minneapolis, MN 55415

Include your name, address, and phone number. As future opportunities arise, we will contact you for more information. We hope that *Beyond Leaf Raking* is just the first of many efforts that will challenge young people to grow through service to others.

---

9 135 PROJECT IDEAS (BEYOND LEAF RAKING)

Young people can play a role in addressing any need or issue that you—or better still, they—identify. As stated in a report from Youth and America's Future: The William T. Grant Foundation Commission on Work, Family, and Citizenship: "There is virtually no limit to what young people—with appropriate education, training, and encouragement—can do, no social need they cannot help meet. We reiterate: Young people are essential resources, and society needs their active participation as citizens."[1]

Thus the possible project ideas are virtually limitless. This chapter presents a collection of ideas arranged by service-related topic. Within each topic, we've tried to include a variety of short-term and long-term, service and justice, at-home and away-from-home projects. As you read them, you probably will think of ten variations and a dozen things youth might learn through the experience. And you can check the resource listing that follows for even more ideas.

Service to Address Hunger, Poverty, and Homelessness

1. Serve in a downtown soup kitchen.
2. Plant gardens with low-income families.
3. Build playground equipment for a low-income day-care center.
4. Go on a mission trip to dig wells for a village.
5. Rehab or build homes for low-income families.
6. Weatherize homes for low-income families.
7. Help staff a food pantry on a regular basis.
8. Work overnight in a homeless shelter.
9. Collect toys for low-income children at Christmas.
10. Gather school supplies for low-income children who are starting school.
11. Organize a food drive for a local food pantry.
12. Lead classes for migrant farm children during the summer.
13. Write letters to advocate for programs to address hunger issues through Bread for the World.
14. Cook a holiday meal for the homeless.
15. Collect books and videos for a church or library in a low-income community.
16. Help food banks or other services with their inventory and bookkeeping.
17. Deliver Meals on Wheels.
18. Do backyard Bible studies for low-income children.
19. Help organize a CROP Walk to raise money for world hunger relief.
20. Form a baby-sitting service to allow low-income mothers to look for jobs or go to school.
21. Spend a week gleaning to get food for a food pantry.
22. Reclaim broken bicycles or lawn mowers and donate them to low-income families.
23. Hold joint parties or picnics with young people from low-income housing in your city.
24. Organize local food merchants to donate food to shelters and food banks.

Service Related to the Environment

25. Spend a week at a cooperative farm.
26. Start, promote, and maintain a church-wide recycling program.
27. Conduct research on a nearby lake or river to determine water quality.
28. Hold a paint-a-thon with other churches to help elderly families, while raising money for projects in the developing world.
29. Plant trees or shrubs at a zoo or park.
30. Form car pools to get to and from youth-group activities.
31. Raise funds to purchase trash cans for a park or recreation area.
32. Befriend a highway by cleaning up litter.
33. Perform energy audits and simple weatherizing for church members.
34. Collect Christmas trees for recycling.
35. Collect phone books for recycling.
36. Research and write articles for your church newsletter about how individuals and families can help to protect the environment.
37. Hold a fund-raiser to buy part of a rainforest, to preserve it from development.
38. Conduct a feasibility study and lobby for a community-wide recycling program, if your community doesn't already have one. (Do the same for your school or church.)

Service with the Elderly

39. Build bird feeders to give to senior citizens.
40. Start an escort service for older church members who need help to get around the church.
41. Bake homemade bread (with an expert) and deliver it to homebound members.
42. Lead recreation in a nursing home.
43. Do fall or spring clean-up for homebound church members. Share refreshments.
44. Interview long-time church members about their stories and make a brochure on the church's history.
45. Record, duplicate, and deliver tapes of the worship service to homebound members.
46. Hold a youth-group/senior-citizen prom.
47. At nursing homes, write or read letters for senior citizens who can no longer write or read.
48. Start a clown troupe to perform in children's homes and nursing homes.
49. Form one-to-one relationships with residents of nursing homes.
50. Help senior citizens with shopping (Christmas, groceries, errands).
51. Offer a fix-up service for simple home repairs for senior citizens.

Service Addressing Race Relations and Multiculturalism

52. Tutor recent immigrants who are learning English.
53. Develop a drama on race relations with a youth group from another ethnic heritage. Present it to congregations in your community.
54. Research and purchase multicultural dolls, toys, and books for day-care centers.
55. Become a partner with a youth group from a congregation with a different racial-ethnic heritage. Organize, do, and debrief service projects together.

Political Action

56. Lobby for equal rights for all people in your community, church, or denomination.
57. Create skits, videos, or music on current issues to raise public awareness.
58. Persuade a local religious radio or television station to have a regular broadcast on youth issues. Produce it.
59. Distribute voter-registration information.
60. Canvass the community to learn about community needs. Tell your findings to the newspaper and city council.
61. Start an "issues alert phone tree" to alert people in the congregation about issues that are being debated in Congress or the state legislature.
62. Write letters to advocate human rights through Amnesty International.
63. Speak at public hearings on issues that affect children and youth.
64. Join efforts to pass legislation that is important to your group.

Service with Children

65. Teach or help with vacation church school in your community or another city.
66. Act as "big buddies" to children who need extra support and role models.
67. Help with or lead an after-school program for children.
68. Produce dramas about current topics to present to children.
69. Coach children in sports.
70. Teach younger children about sexuality from a Christian perspective.
71. Teach arts or crafts to younger children.
72. Lead overnight camping experiences with younger children.
73. Present puppet shows for children in city parks.
74. Read books to children in a library program.
75. Run an after-school program for children.

Service with People Facing Crises

76. Host a carnival for mothers and daughters in a shelter for battered women.
77. Provide blankets, clothing, and other emergency supplies for people caught in a crisis such as a flood, tornado, hurricane, fire, etc.
78. Make "care packages" for teenage mothers, including diapers, baby wipes, baby shampoo, lotion, baby powder, children's books, and a guide for new parents.

Service with Peers

79. Form a Welcome Wagon for new teenagers to your community.
80. Start a peer-ministry program to address the needs and concerns of other teens in the church.
81. Start and staff a "teen talk" hotline for your city.
82. Tutor peers who are having trouble with classes.
83. Form a prayer chain to pray for others in the youth group and school.

Service to Address Violence

84. Form a "mediation squad" to help resolve conflicts in schools or parks.
85. Learn and teach self-defense for women.
86. Learn and teach conflict resolution skills to younger youth.
87. Staff booths at career fairs that promote alternatives to military service.
88. Lobby for tighter restrictions on guns and other weapons.
89. Go on a "relief mission" to a nation that recently experienced war.
90. Protest against injustices in your community.

Service with Prisoners

91. Lead recreation and tutoring in a juvenile center.
92. Hold worship and communion services in prisons.
93. Advocate for humane conditions in prisons.
94. Tutor or train prisoners in job and family skills.
95. Make Christmas stockings for prisoners.
96. Collect books for the prison library.

Service to Protect Animals

97. Help at the local animal shelter.
98. Advocate for humane conditions for livestock.
99. Offer workshops to teach younger children how to care for pets.

Service with People with Disabling Conditions

100. Read written materials for the sightless.
101. Visit institutions for those with mental handicaps.
102. Help with activities in a home for children with disabilities.
103. Offer a shuttle service to help people with disabilities attend church events.
104. Undertake projects to make your church facility accessible to all.
105. Offer tutoring or job-training mentoring to youth with disabilities.
106. Help people with disabilities write letters and send business correspondence.
107. Make special equipment (such as wheelchair ramps) for people with disabilities.
108. Organize campaigns for local businesses and organizations to become accessible.
109. Start an American Sign Language class in the church.
110. Advocate for closed-caption television in your community.

Service Related to Health and Sickness

111. Help Red Cross run a blood drive.
112. Collect medical supplies for overseas missions and relief efforts.
113. Volunteer in an AIDS clinic or hospice.
114. Conduct blood-pressure screenings.
115. Serve candlelight dinners to new parents in the hospital (on their last evening of relative peace!).
116. Visit church members in the hospital. Bring a plant that a group member grew.

Service to Support International Missions

117. Write to missionaries, asking how you could assist in their work.
118. Become a pen pal with a "missionary kid."
119. Welcome furloughing missionaries by purchasing basic food supplies (flour, sugar, etc.)
120. Go on a mission trip to a denominational mission field.

Service to Promote Community Quality

121. Help with safe-driving checkpoints that serve coffee on dangerous holiday weekends.
122. Help nonprofit organizations or the church with big mailings.
123. Design posters for nonprofit organizations.
124. Paint murals over graffiti.
125. Create bike trails in the community.
126. Offer child care during church functions.
127. Create a volunteer guide to nonprofit organizations in your community, listing their purpose, needs, and opportunities.

Service Within the Congregation

128. Send letters to church members on their birthdays.
129. Teach Sunday school.
130. Write and produce a meditation guide for a particular season (Advent, Lent, etc.).
131. Offer child care during a church support group for young parents.
132. Lead in worship.
133. Help prepare and mail the church newsletter.
134. Help church families move.
135. Orchestrate a church clean-up day.

(P.S. Did you notice that we never mentioned raking leaves, though that sometimes might be a good project too?)

Additional Resources

This book has only introduced the many issues, needs, and processes involved in integrating service and Christian education into youth ministry. Here are some of the major resources available to further assist your efforts. Other resources on specific topics can be found in the Notes.

Basics for Service and Learning

The following books are among the most useful in establishing a foundation for service-learning in youth ministry.

Access Guides to Youth Ministry: Justice. Edited by Thomas Bright and John Roberto (New Rochelle, N.Y.: Don Bosco Multimedia, 1990). This collection of essays explores the theory and practice of justice education with youth.

Basic Steps Toward Community Ministry. Carl S. Dudley (Washington, D.C.: Alban Institute, 1991). Written as a guide for church-wide efforts, this book gives practical suggestions for setting up ongoing community ministries. It is particularly useful in helping congregations identify and build on their historical roots for social ministry.

Building Bridges: Teens in Community Service. Eugene C. Roehlkepartain (Minneapolis: RespecTeen, 1992). Written by Search Institute for RespecTeen, this brochure summarizes the value of teen involvement in community service. Available free of charge by calling 1-800-888-3820.

Children as Volunteers: Preparing for Community Service. Rev. ed. Susan J. Ellis, Anne Weisbord, and Katherine H. Noyes (Philadelphia, Penna.: Energize, 1991). If you want to include elementary-age children in service, this booklet is a valuable guide.

Christian Religious Education: Sharing Our Story and Vision. Thomas H. Groome (San Francisco, Cal.: Harper & Row, 1980). This basic text on experienced-based Christian education provides an invaluable reference in connecting service-learning to Christian education. Though academic in tone, the content is highly practical.

Combining Service and Learning: A Resource Book for Community Service and Public Service. 3 vols. Edited by Jane C. Kendall and associates (Raleigh, N.C.: National Society for Experiential Education, 1990). This collection of articles and case studies is indispensable for anyone serious about understanding the history, theory, and practice of service-learning. Volume I focuses on theory; Volume II on practice; and Volume III on resources.

Determining Needs in Your Youth Ministry. Peter L. Benson and Dorothy L. Williams (Loveland, Col.: Group Books, 1987). This guide gives step-by-step instructions for conducting a survey of your youth group to assess needs, concerns, and outlooks. Includes 20 surveys for youth as well as complete scoring and tabulation sheets. A valuable tool for assessing your group's readiness for service-learning. (Available through Search Institute.)

Developing Caring Children. Kate McPherson (Mt. Vernon, Wash.: Project Service Leadership, 1989). This brochure on how to get children involved in service is a valuable introduction for parents and church leaders.

Educating for Peace and Justice. 3 vols. James McGinnis and Kathleen McGinnis et al. (St. Louis, Mo.: Institute for Peace and Justice, 1985). A three-volume set that assists teachers in efforts to teach social issues.

Effective Christian Education: A National Study of Protestant Congregations. Peter L. Benson and Carolyn H. Eklin (Minneapolis, Minn.: Search Institute, 1990). This summary report of a national Search Institute study challenges congregations to rethink their approaches to Christian education for youth and adults.

Experiential Education and the Schools. 2nd ed. Edited by Richard Kraft and James Kielsmeier (Boulder, Col.: Association for Experiential Education, 1986). Though not focused exclusively on service-learning, this collection of articles gives a valuable foundation for the educational side of service-learning.

113

Facts and Faith: A Status Report on Youth Service. Anne C. Lewis (Washington, D.C.: Youth and America's Future: The William T. Grant Foundation Commission on Work, Family, and Citizenship, 1988). This research report is an excellent summary of the impact, practice, and promise of service-learning.

Fund Raisers That Work. Margaret Hinchey (Loveland, Col.: Group Books, 1988). This book contains a wealth of fund-raising ideas for service projects, work camps, and mission trips.

Giving and Volunteering Among American Teenagers 12 to 17 Years of Age. Analyzed by Virginia A. Hodgkinson and Murray S. Weitzman (Washington, D.C.: Independent Sector, 1992). Based on a survey by the Gallup organization, this research report examines the practices, motivations, and experiences of young people who volunteer and donate to charitable causes, including the church.

Growing Hope: A Sourcebook on Integrating Youth Service into the School Curriculum. Edited by Rich Willits Cairns and James C. Kielsmeier (St. Paul, Minn.: National Youth Leadership Council, 1991). This collection of the "best of the best" in service-learning is a key resource. It explores the principles and practices, as well as including numerous case studies from schools across the country.

A Guide for Community Service. Greg Dobie Moser (Morristown, N.J.: Silver Burdette Ginn, 1993). Written explicitly to relate service and learning, this guidebook gives detailed descriptions of 15 youth projects that promote service and social justice. It also includes introductory chapters on theology and the practice of community ministry from a Catholic perspective.

Ideas for Social Action. Anthony Campolo (Grand Rapids, Mich.: Youth Specialties/Zondervan, 1983). For 10 years, youth workers have turned to this resource for guidance on social action in youth ministry. As usual, Campolo makes a provocative case for service and justice involvement, and the "how to" chapters focus on the nuts and bolts of planning projects in youth ministry.

A Kid's Guide to Social Action. Barbara A. Lewis (Minneapolis, Minn.: Free Spirit Publishing, 1991). Give this book to the youth who lead your service projects! It not only gives practical suggestions for ways youth can get involved, but it inspires with dozens of stories of the way youth has made a difference in their communities.

Learning Through Service. Kate McPherson (Mt. Vernon, Wash.: Project Service Leadership, 1989). An exceptional 24-page introduction to the concepts and practical issues in service-learning from one of the experts. Ideal for distributing to your leadership group, your Christian education committee, or your church council, to build an understanding of what you hope to do.

Moving from Awareness to Action on Justice. Network Paper No. 45. Thomas J. Bright (New Rochelle, N.Y.: Don Bosco Multimedia, 1991). Subtitled *Ten Approaches to Involving People in Action for Justice*, this report explores useful strategies for youth ministry.

The Teaching Church: Moving Christian Education to Center Stage. Eugene C. Roehlkepartain (Nashville, Tenn.: Abingdon Press, 1993). This book is the most comprehensive exploration of Search Institute's Effective Christian Education study available. It includes extensive documentation of the urgent need for reform in Christian education.

The Youth Ministry Resource Book. Edited by Eugene C. Roehlkepartain (Loveland, Col.: 1987). Though somewhat dated, this volume describes dozens of social awareness and work camp organizations that serve youth groups. It also includes a comprehensive resource listing of youth-ministry resources on social issues.

Youth Service: A Guidebook for Developing and Operating Effective Programs. Dan Conrad and Diane Hedin (Washington, D.C.: Independent Sector, 1987). These 72 pages are packed with the wisdom and experience of two pioneers in service-learning. Suggested worksheets and exercises make it a particularly useful planning guide.

Project Ideas

Can't think of a project to do? These resources can "prime the pump." Most are written for individual action, but you shouldn't have any trouble translating to groups. The titles are self-explanatory.

Caring for Creation in Your Own Backyard: Over 100 Things Christian Families Can Do to Help the Earth. Loren Wilkinson and Mary Ruth Wilkinson (Ann Arbor, Mich.: Vine Books/Servant Publications, 1992).

50 Simple Things You Can Do to Save the Earth. Earth Works Group (Berkeley, Cal.: Earthworks Press, 1989).

The Helping Hands Handbook: A Guidebook for Kids Who Want to Help People, Animals, and the World We Live In. Patricia Adams and Jean Marzollo (New York, N.Y.: Random House, 1992).

The Kids Can Help Book. Suzanne Logan (New York, N.Y.: Perigee Books, 1992).

Kids Ending Hunger: What Can We Do? Tracy Apple Howard with Sage Howard (Kansas City, Mo.: Andrews & McMeel, 1992).

Save Our Earth: 750 Everyday Ways You Can Help Clean Up the Earth. Diane MacEachern (New York, N.Y.: Dell Publishing, 1990).

Resources for Specific Types of Service

If you become involved in a specific type of community service, these guides give practical help.

The Complete Student Mission Handbook. Ridge Burns with Noel Becchetti (Grand Rapids: Youth Specialties/Zondervan, 1990). A complete guide for overseas mission trips from an evangelical perspective. Includes preparation ideas, fund-raising ideas, and step-by-step processes. Contains little on reflection and debriefing.

Room in the Inn: Ways Your Congregation Can Help Homeless People. Charles F. Strobel (Nashville, Tenn.: Abingdon Press, 1992). This unique guide tells the story of a cooperative project among congregations in Nashville to care for the homeless in empowering and respectful settings. Not only is the book valuable for its step-by-step suggestions, but also for its sensitive guidance on how to relate to homeless people in nonpatronizing ways.

Sharing Groups in Youth Ministry. Walt Marcum (Nashville, Tenn.: Abingdon Press, 1992). A practical manual for youth leaders, including methodology and resources needed to organize and lead youth sharing groups.

Training Teenagers for Peer Ministry. Barbara B. Varenhorst with Lee Sparks (Loveland, Col.: Group Books, 1988). Written by one of the leaders in peer counseling, this guide includes 14 complete training sessions for peer ministry that focus on caring and friendship skills.

The Workcamp Experience: Involving Youth in Outreach to the Needy. John C. Shaw (Loveland, Col.: Group Books, 1987). This detailed book focuses on the step-by-step details of planning a work camp. It is invaluable for people setting up a camp on their own, but has little on reflection and debriefing.

Periodicals

Church and Community Forum. Center for Church and Community Ministries, 5600 S. Woodlawn, Fourth Floor, Chicago, IL 60637. This free newsletter shares insights from the work of the center in parish outreach, service, justice, and renewal of congregational life.

Experiential Education. National Society for Experiential Education, 3509 Haworth Dr., Ste. 207, Raleigh, NC 27609. This bimonthly newsletter for members of the organization covers publications, research, policy, and funding related to experiential education, of which service-learning is one type.

Generator: Journal of Service-Learning and Youth Leadership. National Youth Leadership Council, 1910 W. County Rd. B, St. Paul, MN 55113. This journal explores current thinking and models about service-learning. Includes articles by policy makers, practitioners, and youth.

Peer Update. Augsburg Youth and Family Institute, Augsburg College, 731 21st Ave. South, Minneapolis, MN 55454. A periodic newsletter primarily for individuals who use Barbara Varenhorst's model of peer ministry and peer counseling.

School Youth Service NETWORK. Constitutional Rights Foundation, 601 S. Kingsley Dr., Los Angeles, CA 90005. This quarterly newsletter on school-based programs is free.

Service-Line. Project Service Leadership, 2810 Comanche Dr., Mt. Veron, WA 98273. A newsletter on service-learning published three times per year.

Source Newsletter. Search Institute, 700 S. Third Street, Ste. 210, Minneapolis, MN 55415. This free newsletter is distributed quarterly to provide youth workers with current research about youth today.

Awareness-raising Resources

Though the following resources do not follow the direct-service model for learning about social issues, they can be useful in meetings while preparing for a service project. They also can help with remembering and processing service experience.

Caring for God's Creation. Mike Gillespie (Loveland, Col.: Group Books, 1991). For younger youth, this four-week curriculum is part of Group's Active Bible Curriculum series.

The Compassion Project. Compassion International, 3955 Cragwood Dr., Colorado Springs, CO 80933. A complete kit to teach young people about hunger. Free loan.

CROP Fast. Church World Service, Box 968, Elkhart, IN 46515. A complete kit for an overnight fast to explore hunger issues and raise money for hunger relief.

Food Fast Kit. Global Education Office, Catholic Relief Services, 1011 First Ave., New York, NY 10022. A complete kit for a 24-hour hunger fast.

Homelessness: Activities About People Who Are Homeless. Brethren House Ministries, 6301 56th Ave. North, St. Petersburg, FL 33709. Learning activities and worksheets.

The Joy of Serving. Karen Ceckowski (Loveland, Col.: Group Books, 1991). This four-week curriculum for senior-high groups is a useful introduction to the value of Christian service.

Make a World of Difference: Creative Activities for Global Learning. Rev. ed. (New York, N.Y.: Friendship Press, 1989). About 280 pages of ideas for understanding the world, produced by Church World Service.

Planned Famine. Special Programs, World Vision, 919 W. Huntington Dr., Monrovia, CA 91016; 1-800-445-9887. A weekend hunger-awareness program of fasting, games, film, Bible study, and fund raising.

Service-Learning Organizations

Augsburg Youth and Family Institute. Augsburg College, 731 21st Ave. South, Minneapolis, MN 55454; Ph. 612-330-1624. Offers training and workshops for congregations in peer ministry.

Independent Sector. 1828 L St. N.W., Washington, DC 20036; Ph. 202-223-8100. Broadly focused on philanthropy and volunteerism, the organization publishes resources and research on volunteer and nonprofit management, and a youth service guidebook.

Institute for Peace and Justice. 4144 Lindell, #124, St. Louis, MO 63108; Ph. 314-533-4445. Founded by James and Kathleen McGinnis, this organization publishes a newsletter and supports networking for educators and parents concerned about blending family life and social ministry.

Justice Ministry Services. Center for Youth Ministry Development, Box 699, Naugatuck, NY 06770; Ph. 203-723-1622. Serving leaders in Catholic parishes and schools, this center offers work camps, workshops, training, and resources on the role of justice in faith.

National Center for Service/Learning in Early Adolescence. CASE/CUNY, 25 W. 43rd St., Ste. 612, New York, NY 10036; Ph. 212-642-2946. This organization carris out program development, research, advocacy, and information-sharing to promote service-learning in ways that fit the developmental needs of young adolescents.

National Society for Experiential Education. 3509 Haworth Dr., Ste. 207, Raleigh, NC 27609; Ph. 919-787-3263. The organization serves as a national resource center and professional association of individuals and organizations committed to learning through experience, including service-learning.

National Youth Leadership Council. 1910 W. County Rd. B, St. Paul, MN 55113; Ph. 612-631-3672. NYLC offers membership training for youth and adults, consultation, and resources related to service-learning. It serves as National Serve-America (K–12) Clearinghouse for the Federal Commission on National and Community Service.

Project Service Leadership. 2810 Comanche Dr., Mount Vernon, WA 98273; Ph. 206-428-7614. This resource center helps schools and communities implement service-learning through resources, training, and conferences.

RespecTeen. Lutheran Brotherhood Fraternal Benefit Society, 625 Fourth Ave. South, Minneapolis, MN 55415; 1-800-888-3820. This program seeks to promote the positive development of youth through resources and services for communities. The program is administered through LB's branch system and includes an emphasis on youth service.

Search Institute. 700 S. Third St., Ste. 210, Minneapolis, MN 55415; 1-800-888-7828. Specializing in "practical research benefiting children and youth," this nonprofit organization offers a variety of resources for youth workers in congregations, schools, and communities.

Youth As Resources. National Crime Prevention Council, 1700 K St. N.W., 2nd Fl., Washington, DC 20006; Ph. 202-466-6272. Promotes youth community service by promoting, implementing, and providing materials for youth involvement and crime prevention.

Youth Power! Just Say No International, 2101 Webster St., Ste. 1300, Oakland, CA 94612; Ph. 510-451-6666. This program sponsors service projects to promote, draw on, and encourage skills that help youth cope with adversity. Includes projects that promote drug-free youth, mentoring, peer tutoring, and meeting community needs.

Youth Service America. 1101 15th St. N.W., Ste. 200, Washington, DC 20005; Ph. 202-296-2992. YSA promotes a national network of organizations, programs, and individuals involved in youth community service.

Youth Volunteer Corps of America. 1080 Washington St., Kansas City, MO 64105; Ph. 816-474-5761. This organization is a national network of local programs that assist teens to become involved in community service through intensive summer experiences and short-term projects through the school year. Projects include reflection components.

Major Work Camp Organizations

Dozens of organizations sponsor service projects, work camps, mission trips, and urban experiences for youth groups. Here are some of the national ecumenical/interdenominational programs. Check each one to ensure a good fit with your learning goals and philosophy of ministry. Use the checklist in Figure 10 to evaluate each possible partner.

Appalachia Service Project. 117 W. Watauga, Johnson City, TN 37604; Ph. 615-928-1776.

Group Workcamps. Group Publishing, Box 481, Loveland, CO 80539; Ph. 303-669-3836.

Habitat for Humanity. 121 Habitat St., Americus, GA 31709; Ph. 912-924-6935.

Heifer Project International. Learning and Livestock Center, Rt. 2, Box 33, Perryville, AR 72126; Ph. 501-889-5124.

Inner City Impact. 2704 W. North Ave., Chicago, IL 60647; Ph. 312-384-4200.

International Christian Youth Exchange. 134 W. 26th St., New York, NY 10001; Ph. 212-206-7307.

Mountain TOP. 2704 Twelfth Ave. South, Nashville, TN 37204; Ph. 615-298-1575.

Reach Ministries. Box 1614, Loveland, CO 80539; Ph. 303-667-8932.

Notes

Introduction

1. See Robert N. Bellah et al., *Habits of the Heart* (New York: Harper & Row, 1985).
2. "The Top 5 Challenges Facing Youth Ministry in the '90s," *Group Magazine* (April-May 1991), pp. 29-30.
3. James Kielsmeier, "Reclaiming a Wasted Resource: Youth," *Experiential Education and the Schools* (2nd ed.), ed. Richard Kraft and James Kielsmeier (Boulder, Col.: Association for Experiential Education, 1986), p. 157.
4. For a full discussion of this study, see Eugene C. Roehlkepartain, *The Teaching Church: Moving Christian Education to Center Stage* (Nashville: Abingdon Press, 1993); and Peter L. Benson and Carolyn H. Eklin, *Effective Christian Education: A National Study of Protestant Congregations—Summary Report on Faith, Loyalty, and Congregational Life* (Minneapolis: Search Institute, 1990).
5. Peter L. Benson, *The Troubled Journey: A Portrait of 6th–12th Grade Youth* (Minneapolis: Search Institute, 1993).

Chapter 1. A Call to Service

1. The titles, from several theological perspectives, are almost endless. They include Gustavo Gutiérrez, *A Theology of Liberation* (Maryknoll, N.Y.: Orbis, 1973); Donald B. Kraybill, *The Upside-Down Kingdom* (Scottsdale, Penna.: Herald Press, 1978); Reinhold Niebuhr, *Moral Man and Immoral Society* (New York: Scribner, 1960); Ronald J. Sider, *Rich Christians in an Age of Hunger* (rev. ed.) (Dallas: Word, 1990); Arthur Simon, *Bread for the World* (rev. ed.) (Grand Rapids: Wm. B. Eerdmans, 1984); Tom Sine, *The Mustard-Seed Conspiracy* (Dallas: Word, 1981); Jim Wallis, *Agenda for Biblical People* (New York: Harper & Row, 1976); John Howard Yoder, *The Politics of Jesus* (Grand Rapids: Eerdmans, 1976).
2. Anthony Campolo, *Ideas for Social Action* (El Cajon, Cal.: Youth Specialties, 1983), p. 10.
3. Percentage based on those who said the statement is "a very important benefit to me." *Giving and Volunteering Among American Teenagers 12 to 17 Years of Age: Findings from a National Survey* (Washington, D.C.: Independent Sector, 1992), p. 52. Reprinted with permission.
4. Quoted in Dan Conrad and Diane Hedin, *High School Community Service: A Review of Research and Programs* (Madison, Wis.: National Center on Effective Schools, 1989), p. 27.
5. Dan Conrad and Diane Hedin, "National Assessment of Experiential Education: Summary and Implications," *Experiential Education and the Schools,* ed. Richard Kraft and James Kielsmeier (Boulder, Col.: Association for Experiential Education, 1986), p. 231.
6. Quoted in *Growing Hope: A Sourcebook on Integrating Youth Service into the School Curriculum,* ed. Rich Willits Cairn and James C. Kielsmeier (St. Paul, Minn.: National Youth Leadership Council, 1991), p. 25.
7. In theoretical literature, see, for example, Thomas H. Groome, *Christian Religious Education: Sharing Our Story and Vision* (San Francisco: Harper & Row, 1980).
8. See David Kolb et al., *Organizational Psychology* (Englewood Cliffs, N.J.: Prentice-Hall, 1974).
9. Dan Conrad and Diane Hedin, "Service: A Pathway to Knowledge," *Combining Service and Learning: A Resource Book for Community and Public Service,* vol. 1, ed. Kendall and Associates (Raleigh, N.C.: National Society for Experiential Education, 1990), p. 255.
10. Jane C. Kendall, "Introduction," *Combining Service and Learning,* vol. 1, p. 21.
11. Ibid., pp. 21-22.
12. There are cases when youth services has only a negative impact on those being served. Criticism is well-placed when projects use service recipients as "guinea pigs" who are asked to be grateful for whatever service the young people decide to give. Effective service-learning projects avoid this trap by allowing those in need to define the need and be partners in the effort (chap. 6).
13. John C. Shaw, *The Workcamp Experience: Involving Youth in Outreach to the Needy* (Loveland, Col.: Group Books, 1987), pp. 15-16.
14. Barbara A. Lewis, *The Kid's Guide to Social Action* (Minneapolis: Free Spirit Publishing, 1991), pp. 7-11.
15. *The Forgotten Half: Pathways to Success for America's Youth and Young Families* (Washington, D.C.: Youth and America's Future: The William T. Grant Commission on Work, Family and Citizenship, 1988), p. 79.
16. Quoted in Cairn and Kielsmeier, *Growing Hope,* p. 33.
17. *Giving and Volunteering Among American Teenagers* (Independent Sector), p. 38.
18. *America's Youth 1977–1988,* ed. Robert Bezilla (Princeton, N.J.: The Gallup Organization, 1988), p. 84.
19. George H. Gallup, Jr., and Robert Bezilla, *The Religious Life of Young Americans* (Princeton, N.J.: The George H. Gallup International Institute, 1992), p. 32.
20. Donald G. Elmer, *Revisioning the DRE* (Birmingham, Ala.: Religious Education Press, 1989), p. 59.

Chapter 2. The Impact of Service-Learning

1. News release from the Office of the Press Secretary, The White House, announcing that this group has been named a Daily Point of Light for the Nation (July 22, 1992).
2. Peter L. Benson and Carolyn H. Eklin, *Effective Christian Education: A National Study of Protestant Congregations* (Minneapolis: Search Institute, 1990).
3. Ridge Burns with Noel Becchetti, *The Complete Student Missions Handbook* (Grand Rapids: Youth Specialties/Zondervan, 1990), p. 11.
4. For a full description of the faith-maturity scale, see Benson and Eklin, *Effective Christian Education*, p. 10.
5. Adult faith maturity correlates at .15 for ages 5–12 with frequency of service projects, and at .17 for ages 13–18. In comparison, it correlates at .04 for ages 5–12 with frequency of Sunday school and Bible study, and at .14 for ages 13-18. Finally, it correlates at .06 (ages 5–12) and at .11 (ages 13–18) with frequency of worship attendance.
6. Listed in descending order of strength of correlation. All the correlations are modest, ranging from .24 to .19.
7. Benson and Eklin, *Effective Christian Education*, p. 54.
8. Peter L. Benson and Eugene C. Roehlkepartain, "Kids Who Care: Meeting the Challenge of Youth Service Involvement," *Source Newsletter* (December 1991).
9. Dan Conrad and Diane Hedin, "National Assessment of Experiential Education: Summary and Implications," *Experiential Education and the Schools*, 2nd ed., ed. Richard Kraft and James Kielsmeier (Boulder, Col.: Association for Experiential Eduation, 1986), pp. 229-43.
10. This finding is consistent with other research which shows that attitudes tend to follow behaviors, not vice versa. Interestingly, though, most educational models (including those in the church) first try to change attitudes before asking people to take action.
11. Conrad and Hedin, "National Assessment," pp. 229-43. Also see Faye Caskey, *Model Learner Outcomes for Service-Learning* (St. Paul, Minn.: Minnesota Department of Education, 1991); and *Growing Hope: A Sourcebook on Integrating Youth Service into the School Curriculum*, ed. Rich Willits Cairn and James C. Kielsmeier (St. Paul, Minn.: National Youth Leadership Council, 1991), pp. 18-35.
12. Conrad and Hedin, "National Assessment," p. 231.
13. David Hefferman, *Service Opportunities for Youth* (Washington, D.C.: Children's Defense Fund, 1989), p. 3.
14. Anne Lewis, "Urban Youth in Community Service: Becoming Part of the Solution," *ERIC: Clearinghouse on Urban Education Digest* (September 1992).
15. Ibid.
16. Robert Coles, *The Moral Life of Children* (Boston, Mass.: Houghton Mifflin, 1986), chap. 1.
17. Anthony Campolo, *Growing Up in America: A Sociology of Youth Ministry* (Grand Rapids: Zondervan/Youth Specialties, 1989), p. 153.
18. Faye Caskey, "A Rationale for Service-Learning: Outcomes for Students, School and Community," *Growing Hope*, pp. 25-27.
19. Peter L. Benson, *The Troubled Journey: A Portrait of 6th–12th-Grade Youth* (Minneapolis: Search Institute, 1993), p. 27.

Chapter 3. Ten Questions for Shaping Your Program

1. Carl S. Dudley, "Learnings from the Church and Community Project," *Church and Community Forum* (Spring 1992). Also see Carl S. Dudley, *Basic Steps Toward Community Ministry, Part 2* (Washington, D.C.: Alban Institute, 1991).
2. The most expansive exploring of these images is found in Carl Dudley and Sally A. Johnson, *Energizing the Congregation: Images That Shape Your Church's Ministry* (Louisville, Ky.: Westminster/John Knox, 1993).
3. Carl Dudley and Sally A. Johnson, "Congregational Self Images for Social Ministry," *Carriers of Faith: Lessons From Congregational Studies*, ed. Carl S. Dudley, Jackson W. Carroll, and James P. Wind (Louisville, Ky.: Westminster/John Knox, 1991), p. 112.
4. Ibid., p. 110.
5. Ibid., p. 113.
6. Dudley, *Basic Steps Toward Community Ministry*, pp. 44-45.
7. One resource available to congregations in this regard is *Search Institute Profiles of Congregational Life*. For information, call the Survey Services department at 1-800-888-7828.
8. Peter L. Benson and Carolyn H. Eklin, *Effective Christian Education: A National Study of Protestant Congregations* (Minneapolis: Search Institute, 1990).
9. Virginia A. Hodgkinson, Murray S. Weitzman, and Arthur D. Kirsch, *From Belief to Commitment: The Activities and Finances of Religious Congregations in the United States* (Washington, D.C.: Independent Sector, 1988), p. 18.
10. For information focused specifically on younger youth in service projects, see Joan Schine, *Young Adolescents and Community Service* (Washington, D.C.: Carnegie Council on Adolescent Development, 1989).
11. One useful program for promoting this kind of involvement is the "Speak for Yourself" contest sponsored by the RespecTeen program of Lutheran Brotherhood. Each year, seventh- and eighth-grade students write letters to their members of Congress about issues that concern them. Letters are submitted to a national contest, and winners are chosen to go to Washington to present their case in person. Youth groups can receive a free curriculum guide, with which leaders can guide young people and teach them about the political process. Call RespecTeen at 1-800-888-3820 for deadlines and information.

12. Ridge Burns with Noel Becchetti, *The Complete Student Missions Handbook* (Grand Rapids: Youth Specialties/ Zondervan, 1990), p. 17.

13. Adapted for youth ministry from Dan Conrad and Diane Hedin, *Youth Service: A Guidebook for Developing and Operating Effective Programs* (Washington, D.C.: Independent Sector, 1987), pp. 14-18. Also see Kate McPherson, "Options for Infusing Service into the School Program," *Growing Hope: A Sourcebook on Integrating Youth Service into the School Curriculum*, ed. Rich Willits Cairn and James C. Kielsmeier (St. Paul, Minn.: National Youth Leadership Council, 1991), pp. 37-45. Categories have been renamed to reflect more common terminology in youth ministry.

14. Conrad and Hedin, *Youth Service*, p. 16.

15. Robert Wuthnow, *Acts of Compassion: Caring for Ourselves and Helping Others* (Princeton, N.J.: University Press, 1991), p. 251.

16. Anthony Campolo, *Ideas for Social Action* (El Cajon, Cal.: Youth Specialties, 1983), p. 88.

17. Jane C. Kendall, "A Commentary on Facts and Faith: A Status Report on Youth Service," *Facts and Faith: A Status Report on Youth Service*, ed. Anne C. Lewis (Washington, D.C.: Youth and America's Future: The William T. Grant Foundation Commission on Work, Family and Citizenship, 1988), p. 27.

18. Eugene C. Roehlkepartain, *Youth Ministry in City Churches* (Loveland, Col.: Group Books, 1987), pp. 153-54.

19. Thomas J. Bright, "Moving from Awareness to Action," *Momentum* (November 1992), p. 13.

20. Lyn Baird, "Fanning the Flame," *Experiential Education and the Schools*, ed. Richard Kraft and James Kielsmeier (Boulder, Col.: Association for Experiential Education, 1986), p. 171.

21. Two excellent resources on family involvement in service: Dolores Curran, *Traits of a Healthy Family* (San Francisco: Harper & Row, 1983), chap. 13; and Kathleen McGinnis and James McGinnis, *Parenting for Peace and Justice: Ten Years Later* (Maryknoll, N.Y.: Orbis Books, 1990). Another useful resource: Kate McPherson, *Developing Caring Children* (Mt. Vernon, Wash.: Project Service Leadership, 1989).

Chapter 4. Building Your Program: Choosing a Project

1. Jane C. Kendall, "Introduction," *Combining Service and Learning: A Resource Book for Community and Public Service*, vol. 1, ed. Kendall and Associates (Raleigh, N.C.: National Society for Experiential Education, 1990), pp. 8-10.

2. Robert Greenleaf, *Servant Leadership: A Journey into the Nature of Legitimate Power and Greatness* (New York: Paulist Press, 1977), pp. 13-14.

3. "Principles of Good Practice in Combining Service and Learning," *Combining Service and Learning*, vol. 1, ed. Kendall and Associates, pp. 41-53.

4. Adapted with permission from Kate McPherson, "Educational Leadership for Service-Learning," *Growing Hope: A Sourcebook on Integrating Youth Service into the School Curriculum*, ed. Rich Willits Cairns and James Kielsmeier (St. Paul, Minn.: National Youth Leadership Council, 1991), p. 81.

5. One model for this is presented in Shelby Andress, *Working Together for Youth* (Minneapolis: Lutheran Brotherhood, 1993). Available through Search Institute.

6. Mike Nygren, *Missions and Youth Ministry: The Necessary Love Affair* (Tipp City, Ohio: self-published, n.d.), p. 27.

7. A useful model for assessing needs in community ministry is found in Carl S. Dudley, *Basic Steps Toward Community Ministry* (Washington, D.C.: Alban Institute, 1991). Also see "The Service-Learning Educator: A Guide to Program Management," excerpted in *Combining Service and Learning*, vol. 2, ed. Kendall and Associates, pp. 17-22; and Dan Conrad and Diane Hedin, *Youth Service: A Guidebook for Developing and Operating Effective Programs* (Washington, D.C.: Independent Sector, 1987), pp. 28-31.

Chapter 5. Building Your Program: The Nuts and Bolts

1. One of the most detailed, comprehensive, and applicable sources for planning is found in John C. Shaw, *The Workcamp Experience* (Loveland, Col.: Group Books, 1987).

2. Mike Nygren, *Mission and Youth Ministry: The Necessary Love Affair* (Tipp City, Ohio: self-published, n.d.), p. 29.

3. Based on William R. Ramsay, "Establishing Agency Relationships," *Combining Service and Learning*, vol. 2, ed. Kendall and Associates (Raleigh, N.C.: National Association for Experiential Education, 1990), pp. 109-17. Adapted with the permission of the publisher.

4. "Community Impact Checklist," *Combining Service and Learning*, vol. 2, ed. Kendall and Associates, pp. 267-71.

5. Quoted in Jolene L. Roehlkepartain, "Teens and Trends," *Youth Ministry Bulletin* (January-March 1993).

6. Based on Dan Conrad and Diane Hedin, *Youth Service: A Guidebook for Developing and Operating Effective Programs* (Washington, D.C.: Independent Sector, 1987), p. 35.

7. Quoted in Roehlkepartain, "Teens and Trends."

8. Michael B. Goldstein, "Legal Issues in Combining Service and Learning," *Combining Service and Learning*, vol. 2, ed. Kendall and Associates, pp. 45-47.

9. Conrad and Hedin, *Youth Service*, p. 19.

10. Ibid., p. 32.

11. Nygren, *Mission and Youth Ministry*, p. 28.

12. *Giving and Volunteering Among American Teenagers 12 to 17 Years of Age: Findings from a National Survey* (Washington, D.C.: Independent Sector, 1992), p. 36.

13. See Ridge Burns with Noel Becchetti, *The Complete Student Missions Handbook*, (Grand Rapids: Youth Specialties/Zondervan, 1990), chap. 5.

14. *Giving and Volunteering* (1992), p. 3. For basic information on involving children in appropriate service projects, see Susan J. Ellis, Anne Weisbord, and Katherine H. Noyes, *Children as Volunteers: Preparing for Community Service, Rev. Ed.* (Philadelphia: Energize, 1991).

15. See Barbara Varenhorst with Lee Sparks, *Training Teenagers for Peer Ministry* (Loveland, Col.: Group Books, 1988).

16. Some key resources: Wayne Rice, *Up Close & Personal: How to Build Community in Your Youth Group* (Grand Rapids: Youth Specialties/Zondervan, 1992); Karl Rohnke, *Silver Bullets: A Guide to Initiative Problems, Adventure Games, and Trust Activities* (Dubuque, Iowa: Kendall/Hunt Publishing, 1984); Denny Rydberg, *Building Community in Your Youth Group* (Loveland, Col.: Group Books, 1985);

17. Conrad and Hedin, *Youth Service*, p. 39.

18. Nygren has prepared extensive documentation, job descriptions, history of the Clubhouse program, and the philosophy of ministry. For information, contact Mike Nygren, Ginghamsburg United Methodist Church, 7695 S. County Rd., 25A, Tipp City, OH 45371.

19. Kate McPherson, "Educational Leadership for Service-Learning," *Growing Hope, A Sourcebook on Integrating Youth Service into the School Curriculum,* ed. Rich Willits Cairns and James Kielsmeier (St. Paul, Minn.: National Youth Leadership Council, 1991), p. 87.

Chapter 6. Leadership for Service-Learning

1. Kate McPherson, "Developing Student Ownership: Leadership for Service," *Growing Hope: A Sourcebook on Integrating Youth Service into the School Curriculum*, ed. Rich Willits Cairns and James Kielsmeier (St. Paul, Minn.: National Youth Leadership Council, 1991), p. 72.

2. Ginny Ward Holderness, *Youth Ministry: A New Team Approach* (Atlanta: John Knox, 1981), p. 98.

3. We are indebted to Kate McPherson's extensive work on leadership in service-learning for these role definitions. See her chapter "Educational Leadership for Service-Learning," *Growing Hope.*

4. Combines "interested" and "very interested" responses. Peter L. Benson and Carolyn H. Eklin, *Effective Christian Education: A National Study of Protestant Congregations—A Six-Denomination Report* (Minneapolis: Search Institute, 1990), pp. 47-48.

5. See Kate McPherson, *Developing Ownership for Youth Service Programs* (Mt. Vernon, Wash.: Project Service Leadership, n.d.).

6. Adapted from Kate McPherson, "Educational Leadership for Service-Learning," *Growing Hope*, p. 87.

7. Carl S. Dudley, *Basic Steps Toward Community Ministry* (Washington, D.C.: Alban Institute, 1991), p. 88.

8. Nadinne Cruz, "A Challenge to the Notion of Service," *Combining Service and Learning*, vol. 1, p. 321.

9. Dudley, *Basic Steps*, p. 88.

10. Ibid., p. 89.

11. Greg Druian, Tom Owens, and Sharon Owen, "Experiential Education: A Search For Common Roots," *Experiential Education and the Schools* (2nd ed.), ed. Richard Kraft and James Kielsmeier (Boulder, Col.: Association for Experiential Education, 1986), p. 54.

12. Quoted in McPherson, "Educational Leadership for Service-Learning," *Growing Hope*, p. 96.

13. Ibid., p. 65.

Chapter 7. Structured Reflection: Learning Through Service

1. Thomas H. Groome, *Christian Religious Education: Sharing Our Story and Vision* (San Francisco: Harper & Row, 1980), p. 21.

2. Dan Conrad and Diane Hedin, *Youth Service: A Guidebook for Developing and Operating Effective Programs* (Washington, D.C.: Independent Sector, 1987), p. 39.

3. Groome, *Christian Religious Education*, p. 227.

4. Quoted in *Growing Hope: A Sourcebook on Integrating Youth Service into the School Curriculum*, ed. Rich Willits Cairns and James C. Kielsmeier (St. Paul, Minn.: National Youth Leadership Council, 1991), p. 78.

5. Based on the benefits of reflection outlined in Kate McPherson, *Learning Through Service* (Mt. Vernon, Wash.: Project Service Leadership, 1989), pp. 5-7.

6. See Eugene C. Roehlkepartain, *The Teaching Church: Moving Christian Education to Center Stage* (Nashville: Abingdon Press, 1993), pp. 61-63.

7. Groome, *Christian Religious Education*, p. 253.

8. Barbara Varenhorst, "Discussions with Junior Highers," *Peer Update* (December 1992), p. 6.

9. Groome, *Christian Religious Education*, pp. 208-23. The less technical labels for each of Groome's movements are taken from Thomas Groome, "Using Praxis in Your Classroom," *Youthworker Journal* (Summer 1990), pp. 20-26.

10. Based on Kate McPherson, *Learning Through Service*, p. 4.

11. Based on Glen L. Gish, "The Learning Cycle," *Combining Service and Learning*, vol. 2, ed. Kendall and Associates (Raleigh, N.C.: National Association for Experiential Education, 1990), p. 200. For a more detailed exploration of Kolb's model, see Greig M. Stewart, "Learning Styles as a Filter for Developing Service-Learning Interventions," *Community Service as Values Education*, ed. Cecilia I. Delve et al. (San Francisco: Jossey-Bass, 1990), pp. 31-42. Kolb has developed a "Learning Style Inventory" which allows people to assess and discuss their learning styles. These are available from McBer Company, Training Resource Group, 1137 Newbury St., Boston, MA 02116.

12. Groome, *Christian Religious Education*, p. 208.

13. Larry K. Quinsland and Anne Van Ginkel, "How to Process Experience," *Experiential Education and the Schools* (2nd ed.), ed. Richard Kraft and James Kielsmeier (Boulder, Col.: Association for Experiential Education, 1986), pp. 269-272.

14. McPherson, *Learning Through Service*, pp. 14-15. Used with permission of the author.

15. "Reflecting on What You're Learning," *Combining Service and Learning*, Vol. 2., p. 85.

16. Groome, *Christian Religious Education*, p. 214.

17. Ibid.

18. Ibid., pp. 214-15.

19. See, for example, Dick Murray, *Teaching the Bible to Adults and Youth* (revised and updated) (Nashville: Abingdon Press, 1993).

20. One benefit of coordinating your service-learning effort with the school's efforts could be that your young people would learn these insights from other disciplines through required classwork that builds on their service experience.

21. Groome, *Christian Religious Education*, p. 215.

22. Ibid., p. 217.

23. McPherson, *Learning Through Service*, p. 16.

24. Conrad and Hedin, *Youth Service*, p. 43.

Chapter 9. 135 Project Ideas (Beyond Leaf Raking)

1. *The Forgotten Half: Pathways to Success for America's Youth and Families* (Washington, D.C.: Youth and America's Future: The William T. Grant Foundation Commission on Work, Family, and Citizenship, 1989), p. 79.